THE ENIGMA OF PERCEPTION

McGill-Queen's Studies in the History of Ideas
Series Editor: Philip J. Cercone

THE ENIGMA
OF
PERCEPTION

D.L.C. Maclachlan

McGill-Queen's University Press
Montreal & Kingston • London • Ithaca

© McGill-Queen's University Press 2013
  ISBN 978-0-7735-4141-2 (cloth)
  ISBN 978-0-7735-4142-9 (paper)

Legal deposit second quarter 2013
Bibliothèque nationale du Québec

Printed in Canada on acid-free paper that is 100% ancient forest free
(100% post-consumer recycled), processed chlorine free

This book has been published with the help of a grant from the Canadian
Federation for the Humanities and Social Sciences, through the Awards to
Scholarly Publications Program, using funds provided by the Social Sciences
and Humanities Research Council of Canada.

McGill-Queen's University Press acknowledges the support of the Canada
Council for the Arts for our publishing program. We also acknowledge the
financial support of the Government of Canada through the Canada Book
Fund for our publishing activities.

Library and Archives Canada Cataloguing in Publication

Maclachlan, D.L.C.
  The enigma of perception / D.L.C. Maclachlan.

(McGill-Queen's studies in the history of ideas, 0711-0995; 60)
Includes bibliographical references and index.
ISBN 978-0-7735-4141-2 (bound). – ISBN 978-0-7735-4142-9 (pbk.)

  1. Perception (Philosophy). I. Title. II. Series: McGill-Queen's
studies in the history of ideas; 60

B828.45.M33 2013   121'.34   C2012-908425-5

This book was typeset by Interscript in 10/12 New Baskerville.

On a huge hill,
Cragged and steep, Truth stands, and he that will
Reach her, about must and about must go
And what the hill's suddenness resists, win so.

John Donne
Satire III

Contents

Preface

FOR SEVERAL CENTURIES, since around the time of René Descartes (1596–1650), the causal representative theory was the dominant explanation of perceptual knowledge, and was almost universally accepted among the community of the learned. It is therefore a puzzle that in this present day and age the theory is almost universally rejected. The reason is, of course, that since this theory presupposes a causally organized system of external objects, which produce sensations in us, it cannot be used to explain our original acquisition of a belief in such a world. This looks very much like a fatal flaw; nevertheless, I find it difficult to ignore the attractions of the theory, which made it so popular in the first place.

The solution to the puzzle is to recognize that although the pattern of inference at the heart of the causal representative theory depends on large assumptions, which preclude the theory from offering an explanation of the original acquisition of perceptual knowledge, nevertheless these assumptions about an external world governed by causal law are generally accepted as true, even by Hume the Sceptic. This means that it cannot be illegitimate to operate the pattern of inference which the theory involves. If the assumptions required were false, that would be the end of the matter – but they are not!

The theory does indeed make a further claim which is more controversial. It assumes that it is possible to describe and make judgments about the sensations produced in us by the external objects. This would be challenged by supporters of the private language argument, and I devote a substantial chapter to answering that argument.

If the necessary assumptions can all be put in place, the traditional causal representative theory of perception can be brought back, albeit in a reduced form. It is no doubt a disappointment to concede that the theory cannot explain our original knowledge of the external world, but at least the pattern of inference is available on a second pass to offer some justification or correction for perceptual beliefs first acquired in some other way. One important result emerging from this second pass is the essential validation of John Locke's celebrated distinction between primary and secondary qualities. Associated with this, we have permission to redescribe the external causes of our sensations in whatever terms seem appropriate to our most advanced scientific theories.

We are still left with the problem of explaining how we form our original conception of the external physical world which is presupposed by the causal representative theory. I shall attempt to deal with the problem in the second part of this work. Even if it is thought that I have completely failed, this will not affect the argument of the first part. Whatever account may be offered of our original acquisition of perceptual knowledge, even if one believes that no acceptable account has or can be found, the second pass offered by the traditional theory will remain a legitimate pattern of inference.

It is clear that our beliefs about the world in which we live are based, somehow or other, on a sensory input which comes from the external objects. The problem of perception is to explicate this "somehow or other." How we accomplish the feat is not clear and not agreed. We may want to say that our knowledge of the external world is somehow caused by the stimulation of the senses, but we come up against the problem that the cause and the effect belong to different conceptual systems. Our knowledge of the world belongs to what Wilfrid Sellars called the "space of reasons," whereas the physiological processes on which it is based belong to the natural order. It seems impossible to connect the two components, whether we work from the bottom up, beginning with the physiology, or from the top down, beginning with the mature knowledge and trying to strip away the elements of inference involved.

My solution is to accept the causal connection, but to offer a radical re-interpretation of its nature. I can use the notion of information to explain my point. I distinguish between the *transmission* of information involved in normal causality and the *extraction* of information, which is the essence of cognition. The extraction of information is the response of the cognitive subject to what is being supplied by the antecedent universe. This does, indeed, require a robust conception of the cognitive subject as an active being combining a given manifold. The response of the subject to the incoming data can be regarded as a kind of causal connection, so long as we realize that the activity grounding the connection lies in the effect and not in the cause. As the act of the cognitive subject, the response to the given manifold must have a purpose. I submit that the purpose is to use the information extracted to represent reality in order to guide the decisions of the agent. The adoption of such a purpose involves, of course, a conception of the reality to be rep-resented. This a priori conception of reality does not, indeed, introduce any kind of object: I shall argue that "reality" is a mass term and not a count noun.

The representation of reality involves the use of what F.H. Bradley calls "logical ideas" and contrasts with "psychological ideas," which are mental particulars (I follow Bradley rather than Gottlob Frege, who supple-ments psychological ideas with the senses attached to signs). These "logi-cal ideas" or "ideal contents" have a built-in generality which permits their use in a variety of acts of representation. Our familiar "concepts" are certainly logical ideas in Bradley's sense, but so also are maps and the "scenarios" introduced by Christopher Peacocke, which have the requi-site generality. Perhaps we should distinguish between a narrow sense in which concepts are associated with the use of language and a broad sense in which concepts are used to guide behaviour. I speculate that concepts in this broad sense are more primitive than the scenarios which are so prominent in consciousness. These prominent sensory represen-tations appear at a later stage, perhaps associated with the development of the cerebral cortex.

The reality we presuppose has parts distinguished through represen-tations of space and time. I take the idea of the future as particularly fundamental, because of its connection with the actions we envisage. I even suggest that perception is essentially perception of the future. This idea definitely separates the object of perception from the perceptual experience, since the experience is in the present and the object is in the future!

I also include a review of the neglected theory proposed by James J. Gibson almost fifty years ago. Gibson's central idea is that there is an in-formation flow from the ambient universe. Gibson's important distinc-tion introduces the extraction of values for higher-order variables, such as ratios and proportions, which do not necessarily change with a change in our raw experiences. This distinction ties together the two parts of my book. The ratios that persist as I move through the world to pick up in-formation are the basis for the concepts originally used in perceptual cognition; the more detailed information that changes as I change my position is still available in experience and can be exploited in a second pass through an inference to its cause.

I offer a brief discussion of internalism and externalism to show how this thorny philosophical problem can be handled, using the resources of the theory developed in this book. I conclude by comparing and con-trasting my theory with the position David Chalmers expressed in his recent book *The Character of Consciousness*. We are both champions of phenomenal realism, and we both recognize the importance of the scientific facts that energized the causal representative theory. I argue, however, that I have a better way of integrating these facts.

I have been struggling for many years with the problem of perception, which I have now promoted to the rank of an enigma. During this long struggle, I have received help from a huge number and variety of sources. I fear that to provide a complete list would be well beyond my powers, and I have decided not to attempt it. This does not mean that I think that I have done this all by myself or that I am not grateful to those who have helped. I must, however, acknowledge a grant which has made possible the publication of this work. This book has been published with the help of a grant from the Canadian Federation for the Humanities and Social Sciences, through the Awards to Scholarly Publications Program, using funds provided by the Social Sciences and Humanities Research Council of Canada.

PART ONE

1

The Traditional Theory Demolished

1 THE TRADITIONAL THEORY OF PERCEPTION

Perception is the process by which somehow or other we acquire beliefs about the external world on the basis of an input from that external world, fed in through the senses. This is an account with which, I imagine, virtually everyone would be in essential agreement. The differences break out when we try to put clothes on the bare idea of "somehow or other." Although the general theory of perception I have outlined is accepted by almost everyone who thinks about these matters today, it is not true that there is no alternative. There may be no *reasonable* alternative today, with all our knowledge about the propagation of light and human physiology, but this was not the case in the ancient world before the rise of modern science. There was at one time an alternative theory, intuitively plausible, which was based on the use of our hands and bodies in the exploration of the world. We are equipped with feelers (also known as hands) with which we can lay hold of things in the vicinity. We gain knowledge of such things by grasping them in a quite literal sense. We can also make contact with external objects by using other parts of the body. This was the system used by Dr Johnson when he refuted Bishop Berkeley by kicking the stone. Although vestiges of this theory persist in metaphors we use in discussing perception, such as "apprehend," the theory is no longer serious competition.

Things were very different, of course, in ancient Greece, where the variety of available theories was much greater. Visual perception was a special problem because the objects perceived were at a distance from the eye. Ruling out the possibility of action at a distance, how was the physical connection necessary for perception to be explained? There were two options: either information was conveyed by something leaving the object and reaching the eye, or else something emerged from the eye to reach the surface of the object, gathering in this way the available information. We now know that the idea of fiery rays coming from the eye to illuminate the object is a complete myth, and we accept the competing idea that visual perception involves light rays reflected from the object and entering the eye.[1]

Although the central problem that worried the Greeks has now been settled, there is one aspect that remains as mysterious as ever. How in detail do we get from the manifold input impacting the sensory system to the very extensive system of beliefs constituting our knowledge of the external world? We can anticipate that this is going to be a truly formidable problem once we recognize that we begin with physiological processes in the nervous system, initiated by various kinds of physical stimulation, and end up with a set of beliefs described through a radically different conceptual scheme. Before we gear up for an attack on this central difficulty, there is another problem, which may appear more urgent. The beliefs we acquire through the senses are used to guide our actions, to achieve our objectives, and to avoid the dangers that threaten us; but as everybody knows, including Descartes, the beliefs about the world that we acquire through perception are not entirely reliable. When used to guide behaviour, they sometimes lead to disaster. We are therefore most anxious, particularly in cases where we have our doubts, to find ways of either justifying or correcting our original beliefs.

Sometimes, we justify the original claim by carrying out further observations. I can verify my claim that there is a desk in front of my eyes, supplementing my visual experience by the use of my hands to confirm that there is a solid object in front of me. In this case the further test looks a bit like overkill, but it can carried out, and there are many cases when such tests are worthwhile and even important. Macbeth obviously thought so when he said: "Is this a dagger which I see before me, / The handle toward my hand? Come, let me clutch thee. / I have thee not, and yet I see thee still."[2]

To take another example, I see before me a glass containing a colourless, odourless liquid that I believe to be water. To check my belief, I submit it to the taste test, since orthodox science defines water as tasteless, as well as colourless and odourless. The taste that I get when I sip the liquid will confirm or refute my original belief. It is not, of course,

1 Many ancient philosophers, such as Galen, adopted a compromise between these two alternatives, combining emissions from the eye with the light emitted by the sun. See the discussion of this material provided by A. Mark Smith, *Ptolemy and the Foundations of Ancient Mathematical Optics*, section 1, 23–30.

2 William Shakespeare, *Macbeth*, act 2, scene 1, ll. 34–6.

necessary to use a *different* sense to confirm a belief. I can confirm what I think I see by taking another look, perhaps varying the conditions of observation. I can improve the lighting or I can change my point of view. When I change my point of view there will be a change in the way the thing looks, but how the thing looks from a different point of view may simply confirm my original belief about what the thing is.[3]

Another way to confirm or correct a belief about the nature of a thing is by observing its effects on other things. The temperance lecturer drops a worm into each of two glasses of clear liquid. In the one, the worm writhes and shrivels; in the other, it swims around and has a good time. We now know which glass contains the water and which has the gin. Sometimes, the effect from which I infer the character of the object is an effect on myself. I perceive that a piece of iron is hot, very hot, when it glows red. When it is not glowing, I tend to believe that it is not hot. I can test this belief by touching it with my finger (not necessarily recommended). From the blister it raises, I can infer that the metal was hot after all. Before I get around to this inference, however, I have a more immediate reason to believe that the iron was hotter than it looked. This is the sensation of pain I experience when I touch the metal, which I attribute to its very high temperature. I infer the condition of the object responsible from the sensation it produces in me.

This kind of case is a special form of the general practice of inferring causes from effects and was used as a model to introduce the traditional theory of perception. In less extreme cases, the piece of metal sometimes feels cold and sometimes warm to the touch. Here, too, we experience sensations from which we infer the temperature of the object. We do have to be careful, since the sensations are conditioned by the state of the hand employed as well as by the state of the object. This is shown by the famous experiment of the three bowls of water. Arrange three bowls in a row, with cold water in the one on the left, hot water on the right, and lukewarm water in the middle bowl. Put the left hand in the cold water and the right hand in the hot water. Then test the water in the middle. The sensation we get through the left hand is quite different from the sensation which we get through the right hand. But it is the same lukewarm water which feels warm to the hand from the cold water and cool to the hand from the hot water.[4]

---

3 Notice that changing my point of view may provide fresh information about *where* the thing is!

4 It turns out that the sensation of heat we experience is more closely correlated with the *flow* of heat from the object to the body rather than its absolute temperature.

After this, it is easy to argue that experienced tastes and smells are also sensations produced in us by molecules detaching from the objects affecting the appropriate organs. Again, the smells and tastes experienced can be shown to be a function of both the arriving molecules and the condition of the sensory apparatus. We can often identify the thing we are tasting or the thing making the smell from the sensations that we experience.

Hearing is the next sense to fall to this analysis. We must distinguish between the sounds heard and the sound waves which strike the ear. The barking dog produces sound waves, which travel to the ear and, through complicated physiological processes, generate the sounds we hear. The tree that falls to the ground in a deserted forest makes sound waves, but there are no sensations of sound if there is no one to hear them. From the nature of the sounds we hear, we can infer the things responsible on the basis of our past experience of what usually make these kinds of sounds.

Traditional philosophers met with more resistance when they attempted to bring into this system the sense of sight. It seems odd to describe the visual display as a sensation – it is more comfortable to talk about it as the way things look or appear. Nevertheless, the visual presentation is clearly a function of the real external objects that populate space together with the conditions of observation. That which is directly experienced changes when we change our point of view without any change in the real physical world. Therefore, what is experienced is not the physical world as it is in itself, but visual sensations produced in us by light coming from the physical objects and striking the eye, just as auditory sensations are produced in us by sound waves striking the ear.[5] To call the visual display a sensation is indeed to stretch the word way beyond its normal use. But this step can be justified by noting that in all cases the immediate presentation is an effect produced in us by the object, together with certain intervening conditions whose variation reveals the distinction between the sensation and the external thing. This wide sense of sensation Immanuel Kant defines in the *Critique of Pure Reason* as "the effect of an object on the faculty of representation" (B34 A20). If one still has scruples about calling the visual content present in immediate experience *sensation,* this is no great matter, so long as one recognizes that this content has been generated through the impact of light waves on the visual system. This is all that is needed to permit an inference to the external cause, and the use of the actual word "sensation" is not required.

5 For a detailed discussion of this analogy, see D.L.C. Maclachlan, *Philosophy of Perception,* chapter 5.

We are now close to the traditional theory of double existence, as Hume calls it. We must distinguish between sensations, or impressions, or whatever, which are immediately present in consciousness, and the physical objects that exist in an external world. There is a causal relation between the sensations and the physical objects by which they are produced. It is therefore possible to infer the character of the objects from the sensations experienced, making allowance for the distortions introduced by the conditions of observation. It is also possible to predict what sensations are likely to be experienced in the future if we deploy our observational systems in the appropriate manner and the world develops as we think it should.

This all looks extremely plausible, and it now seems that we have a solution to the basic problem of perception with which we began. We now know, it seems, how we acquire perceptual beliefs about an external world. We make inferences from the sensations external things produce in us.[6] This is the theory David Hume identified as the "doctrine of the learned," and it has been so widely accepted since the time of Descartes that it may be fairly regarded as the traditional theory of perception.

It may be suggested that to reduce sensory experience to sensations or impressions in this way is a serious oversimplification. Sense experience may be thought to have an internal structure, involving, for instance, an act of experiencing and the content of that act, which might even be taken as the representation of some object. Such distinctions will become important in the second part of this work, when we are forced to try an alternative to the traditional theory. Working with the causal theory of perception, however, such complications can be ignored. So long as we have inner items that are separate existences causally correlated with external objects, we need not trouble ourselves with further questions about the nature of these inner effects. We have what we need to infer the causes in the external world from the effects in the mind, which is the modus operandi of the traditional causal theory of perception.

2 THE ACHILLES' HEEL OF THE TRADITIONAL STORY

It is quite clear, however, that this traditional theory is not going to work. The theory depends upon inferences from particular sensations to their external causes. This pattern of inference can develop only *after* a belief in a system of causally connected physical objects is already in place, and

---

6 It is true enough that we do not notice we are making these inferences all the time, but it would not be normal to focus on the inferential process, when our interest is in the conclusion.

so it cannot be used to explain how we originally reach such a belief. The explanation is circular, presupposing what it seeks to explain. Sensations are understood as effects produced in us by external objects, but if all we can access are the sensations, then how can we know that they are produced by external causes?

The traditional theory of perception had its grip upon the imagination because it developed in a context in which the concern was to confirm or correct beliefs about the external world, which are known to be not entirely reliable.[7] Causal reasoning can be used to distinguish things through their different effects on other things, even if they originally seemed to be similar. The main innovation in the traditional theory was to introduce a special class of effects produced in the conscious experience of the cognitive subject. Following Kant, we can define these effects as "sensations." From these effects, we can infer the nature of the causes which produce them, in much the same way as we use the effects of an object on other things to infer its character.

Thus, the story I have been telling was developed in a context in which physical objects in a causal system were taken for granted. Also assumed was a power of causal reasoning through which we could infer effects from their causes and causes from their effects. The addition to the standard account of the physical world in the new theory was the introduction of sensations in the wide sense, which are conceived as the effects in conscious experience of the external objects, operating through the sensory systems of the perceiver.

If we are to improve our knowledge of things in the world by making inferences from their effects on other things, it is, of course, essential to be able to detect the nature of these effects. We must be able to make judgments about the changes that have taken place. There is no point in using litmus paper to test a solution unless we are able to judge when the paper changes colour. In the same way, if we are to use our sensations to refine our knowledge of their external causes, it must be possible to make judgments about the character of these sensations. This requires an experiencing and cognitive subject capable of accessing the effects produced in consciousness by the external causes. This subject must be able to combine in one consciousness the manifold of sensations, and to compare and contrast them with one another. Moreover, the subject must be able to introduce concepts which make possible the judgments through which the nature of the sensations can be described.

---

7 This is certainly the focus at the opening of Descartes' *Meditations on First Philosophy*.

It is not enough, then, to have sensations or impressions forming a bundle in consciousness – these effects of external causes must be objects of cognition that can be described through acts of judgment performed by the cognitive subject. This focus on the status of the inner elements as objects of cognition was perhaps responsible for the introduction of the new term "sense-datum" at the beginning of the last century. Many philosophers began to change their way of thinking and talking about the items immediately present to the mind, formerly known as sensations. The new term "sense-datum" emphasized that the inner elements were objects or data for the cognitive subject, while breaking any conceptual tie to an external cause associated with the idea of sensation. If a sensation is understood in line with Kant's definition as the effect of the object on the cognitive subject, then a link to the external cause is built into the very notion (this is even clearer with the Humean term "impression"). The term "sense-datum" was introduced to avoid begging the question about a link to causes in the external world which may or may not exist. This gave new life to traditional worries about the existence of the external world.

3 THE CHALLENGE OF THE SCEPTIC

As we have seen, the traditional theory of perception cannot be used to explain or justify our original belief in an external world and the various things which populate it. This does not mean that we must necessarily give up our natural belief in a reality beyond the mind, since we cannot rule out the possibility that this belief is legitimately acquired in some other way. The sceptic, however, does rule out any such possibility. We tend to think of the smells and sounds we experience as sensations produced in the mind by external causes. A certain smell is produced by a skunk, a certain sound by a barking dog. But if we are not allowed to infer the skunk from the smell and the dog from the sound, how can we know that these animals are in the vicinity? Once inference to external causes is demolished as the original source of our knowledge, how can we have the temerity to suggest some other mysterious way of getting to the external world? It seems that I have no reason to believe in anything except the sense-data immediately present in my consciousness, and to persist in beliefs about things beyond is contrary to reason. The only completely rational theory is solipsism of the present moment. Nothing exists except my own self and my sense-data.

Perhaps we can avoid this collapse into solipsism by considering the theory put forward by Berkeley at the beginning of the eighteenth century. According to Berkeley the ideas or sensations found in experience are produced not by material things in an external world but by God Himself. This allows Berkeley to distinguish between chimeras of the imagination and real things. Real things, like apples and pears, are collections of ideas in the mind of God, and we perceive real things when God provides us with a sample from his extensive collection. We do not perceive real things when we strike out on our own and produce in imagination ideas not sanctioned by the Deity.

This theory has certain attractions if we already believe in the existence of a God who has created the universe of material things, which are supposed to produce ideas in us. It allows us to cut out the middleman, with God directly providing the ideas representing real things. But this theory will not satisfy the determined sceptic, who dismisses both the material universe and the existence of God. I can be sure of nothing but my own existence and the immediate contents of my consciousness. There seem to be no grounds for believing in anything else supposed to be the cause of the immediate presentations. After all, we acknowledge occasional hallucinations – like the one that troubled Macbeth. Also, there are dreams. Perhaps life is but a dream!

The very structure of the sense-datum theory has made it harder to dispel what might otherwise be vague worries that complete hallucinations are more widespread than we normally think. The sense-datum theory replaces the awareness of external objects with an awareness of internal objects. The model transfers a conceptual scheme from its ordinary use where we experience and make judgments about external objects to a new use where we experience and make judgments about internal objects – the sense-data. Instead of: "We see tables and chairs," we get: "We see sense-data."[8] We may feel some uneasiness about moving the application of the conceptual scheme in so dramatic a fashion, but sense-datum philosophers might argue that the scheme does not work very well in its original setting, since it presupposes a direct cognitive access to the external objects thought to be experienced. In view of the many factors lying between the centre of experience in the brain and the external objects, even those which are close by, this direct access is hard to understand and would be possible only through some miracle.[9] On the other hand, direct access to sense-data produced in one's own

8 To avoid the objection that seeing involves the use of the eyes, etc., the more cautious might rephrase this as the move from: "We have a visual awareness of tables and chairs" to "We have a visual awareness of sense-data."

9 Malebranche, for instance, ridicules the notion "that the soul should leave the body to stroll about the heavens ... to behold the sun, the stars and an infinity of objects external to us." See the discussion in John W. Yolton, *Perception and Reality*, 85–6.

mind makes perfect sense. The conceptual scheme employed in our ordinary thinking becomes truly coherent only when its application is moved within the mind.

The awareness of these sense-data is *virtually* infallible and incorrigible, which compares favourably with the sometimes shaky claims to see physical objects that we make in ordinary life. The idea that judgments about sense-data must be infallible and incorrigible derives largely from the Cartesian search for certainty in the foundation of knowledge. The qualification "virtually" is there, because I am unable to rule out the possibility of a certain level of bungling in the conceptualization of the sense-data. Gareth Evans gives the example of seeing "ten points of light arranged in a circle."[10] Apart from mistakes about the *sources* of light due to mirrors, etc., it is also quite possible to make a mistake about the number of points in immediate experience and hence to misdescribe the sense-datum.

It may be hard to suppose that the sounds and smells we experience immediately, now called "sense-data," come to us out of the blue; we naturally assume that they are effects produced in the mind by external causes which may be inferred from the effects they produce. The problem is that although we know in our hearts that the sense-data are sensations, produced in the mind by external causes, the sense-datum theory has been constructed in such a way that we are forced to disallow this vital piece of evidence. All we are given are the sense-data that we can compare and contrast and conceptualize, but there is no imaginable route to anything beyond the domain of sense-data. We cannot imagine how it is possible to have an immediate awareness of external objects of the kind we enjoy in our consciousness of sense-data.[11] If such an awareness is necessary for knowledge, then there can be no knowledge of an external world.

The essential difficulty with the sense-datum theory is that the theory makes no provision for objects of cognition other than the sense-data themselves. It may well be that the concept of direct acquaintance, which lies at the heart of the sense-datum theory, originates in the naive realist belief that we are directly acquainted with the commonsense physical objects which come within the range of our senses; but on reflection such a cognitive relation seems unintelligible unless its objects are restricted to the sense-data that appear in the

---

10 See Gareth Evans, *The Varieties of Reference,* 228–9.
11 See the worry expressed by Malebranche in note 9 above.

mind.[12] Thus, the problem is not simply that we can find no secure
justification for inferences to a physical world that transcends these
sense-data, since without access to the external causes we cannot establish the correlations which ground such inferences – the problem
is much, much worse. If the system does not allow access to external
objects then there is no place within it for the physical world as a
whole, or for any of its parts. Such a transcendent reality is literally
unthinkable: we cannot say that it exists, or that it does not exist.
Whereof one cannot speak, thereof one must be silent.

If we cannot have a genuine external reality, then an attempt must
be made to produce a reasonable facsimile in order to avoid too great
a disruption in our normal patterns of thought. Berkeley met this re-
quirement for his theory when he interpreted our commonsense physical objects as collections of ideas in the mind of God. A.J. Ayer tried to do
the same thing for sense-data during his early *phenomenalist* phase.[13]
Unlike Berkeley, Ayer did not have available a divine mind to house the
collections of ideas constituting physical objects. Ayer had a much harder
struggle. It was necessary to supplement *actual* sense-data with *possible*
sense-data, so that the elephant in the room could be defined as a collection of actual and possible sense-data. This suggestion had many difficulties and few supporters, not even in its heyday. Ayer devised an ingenious
version of the theory according to which categorical statements about
physical objects were replaced by sets of hypothetical statements about
sense-data. The simple statement that there is a table in the next room is
to be replaced by a set of statements about the sense-data to be experienced if certain conditions are satisfied (one such condition would be
described in ordinary language as "going into the next room to look").
This would seem to be circular. We accept the statements about possible
sense-data, because we believe that there is a table in the next room. Even
this clever version of the theory attracted derision rather than converts.

The theory of phenomenalism is now so dead that it was perhaps not
necessary to mention it, and I am certainly not going to spend the time
working through the details of the objections that brought the theory
down. Even H.H. Price, who was very much in the grip of the sense-
datum model, finally breaks ranks and introduces what he calls the

12 To think of the sense-data as items which appear *in the mind* is actually a survival
from earlier dualist patterns of thought according to which sense-data are conceived as
sensations which are the effects in the mind of external objects. For the rigorous champion
of sense-data, these items are neither mental nor physical – they are just there, like Mount
Everest!

13 A.J. Ayer, *The Foundations of Empirical Knowledge.*

"physical occupant," which is posited a priori. There is a notion of material thinghood that is for Price "an *a priori* notion, which cannot be reached by inspection of sense-data and abstraction of their common characteristics."[14]

The key assumption in the sense-datum model is that the only way to acquire knowledge of particular things is through what Bertrand Russell calls a "singular thought" involving a direct acquaintance with some object.[15] Although we may naively suppose that we have such a cognitive relation to the commonsense material objects in the external world, it is difficult to believe that this is really possible. The only items with which we are directly acquainted are the sense-data, such as the sounds and smells that are immediately present in consciousness. It is because we do have a direct experience of sense-data *inside* the mind that we can imagine a direct experience of physical objects *outside* the mind.[16] When we recognize that this is not possible, we try to infer the external objects from the sense-data directly presented. When this does not work, we may capitulate and, as Hume suggests, go off to play backgammon.

What is being assumed in this kind of defeatism is that there is no other possible route to knowledge apart from direct awareness or inference. But we must assume some other way, even if we are not able at the moment to explain what it is. Otherwise, belief in an external world would have to be given up. Indeed, the thesis that commonsense physical objects cannot be reached by either direct awareness or inference presupposes some other way of introducing the physical objects, since they are not to be accessed in either of the ways suggested.

4 BLINDSIGHT

The idea that our original beliefs about the external world must depend on an inference from sensations immediately present in experience has also been undermined in recent years by important empirical evidence. This is the evidence of what is called "blindsight," which would have shaken the supporters of the traditional theory had knowledge of it been

14 H.H. Price, *Perception*, 306.

15 Bertrand Russell, *Problems of Philosophy*, chapter 5. There is a more detailed account of Russell's conception of direct acquaintance and singular thoughts at the beginning of chapter 5.

16 I suggested earlier that the sense-datum theory was introduced through transferring a familiar model of direct perception from the external to the internal domain. This is not incompatible with the further claim that we *imagine* a direct perception of external objects because we *do have* a direct experience of internal objects.

available at the time. Blindsight occurs in individuals who have completely lost visual experience in the usual sense, due to the destruction of the visual cortex, perhaps by a stroke. Some such individuals have demonstrated an uncanny capacity to register the nature of their environment through the use of visual input. A most impressive case was reported in the *New York Times*[17] where the subject navigates a cluttered obstacle course, although he claims that he couldn't see a thing. This was not indeed a total mystery, since the eyes were undamaged and were sending signals to primitive, subcortical regions of the brain. But the knowledge of the environment that allowed the subject to thread his way past the garbage can and the tripod was not based on an inference from visual sensations, since there were *no* visual sensations.

This unusual case is important, because it is so clear-cut. It can be supported, however, by an array of vaguer arguments. It seems to me, for instance, that when a rock is thrown at my head, I take rapid evasive action without consciously registering the appropriate visual sensation. Moreover, the haptic sensory system, which we use when groping about in the dark, has always been a worry for the traditional theory; even if some sensations may be found here and there, the haptic system does not seem to provide us with the organized sensory representation we get in the case of sight. Sight provides us with a well-defined visual display that changes systematically when we move our bodies, our heads, or our eyes. It is worth noting that corresponding to blindsight there are also cases of what may be called "deafhearing," where the subject is able to extract information from auditory stimulation while denying any experience of sound. Again, the explanation is that damage to the brain has disrupted the normal experiential system.[18]

Thus, it looks as if we *do not* always use an inference from given sensations to acquire our knowledge of the external world. When this is added to the earlier argument that we *could not* originally acquire our knowledge of the physical world through an inference from sensations, it is difficult to deny the collapse of the traditional explanation of perceptual knowledge as a system of inferences from given sensations to their external causes. What is so frustrating is that if we could find a path from the system of sense-data to the system of physical objects, then we could integrate the sense-data as effects produced by the physical objects. But we have no grounds for treating the sense-data as effects of external causes

17 23 December 2008.

18 Cf. Maria Mozaz Garde and Alan Cowey, "'Deaf Hearing': Unacknowledged Detection of Auditory Stimuli in a Patient with Cerebral Deafness," *Cortex* 36, no. 1 (2000): 71–9.

until we construct the system of the physical world, and hence this idea cannot be presupposed in the construction of the physical system. The Achilles' heel of the traditional theory, then, is that it must assume what it is supposed to prove. It cannot be used to explain how we acquire our original knowledge of the external world, because the inferences from sensations on which it depends cannot be operated until the knowledge of a system of external objects ruled by causal law is already in place.

2

The Traditional Theory Comes Back to Life

1 HOW TO RESURRECT THE TRADITIONAL THEORY

If the assumptions on which the traditional theory depends were thought to be false, this would be the end of the matter. The received wisdom, however, is that these assumptions are *not* false. Not even Hume the Sceptic wishes to abandon our belief in a causally organized system of physical objects. As he remarks in the *Treatise*: "it is in vain to ask, *Whether there be body or not?* That is a point which we must take for granted in all our reasonings."[1] If the belief in a system of causally organized physical objects in space and time is not false, then it cannot be illegitimate to operate the pattern of inference at the heart of the causal representative theory. It depends on an assumption, but the assumption is *true*!

The way is perhaps now open to retrieve what remains valid in the traditional theory of perception. Once the fatal flaw is discovered, the temptation is to consign the theory to the dustbin of history and think no more about it. But it is hard to believe that a theory that was so widely accepted for so many years by so many eminent philosophers does not contain some element of truth. Certainly, we must abandon the claim that this is *the* way in which we acquire knowledge of the external world. The phenomenon of blindsight establishes conclusively that it is not the *only* way. There are other ways of obtaining information about the environment which do not involve an inference from sensations. But this does not make it illegitimate to infer from effects in us to external causes. This pattern of inference was introduced to confirm or correct our natural beliefs about the world in which we live, since we found that these beliefs were not entirely reliable. Certainly, the idea that we directly experience sensations, effects produced in us by antecedent physiological

1 David Hume, *Treatise on Human Nature*, 187.

causes, solves at a stroke the many puzzles associated with perceptual error, including illusion and hallucination. The man who thinks he is seeing pink elephants has the appropriate visual sensations, although in this case they are caused not by real pink elephants but by the drink.

2 THE SPACE OF REASONS

The operation introduced in the traditional theory can be conceived as a kind of second pass through which we review our original naive beliefs about the world around us. If this is what it is, these inferences from sensations cannot be used to explain our original acquisition of the beliefs which we are now reviewing. We do not reach our original beliefs about the external world by an inference from sensations, but in some other way.

The traditional theory of perception has its smooth plausibility, because it operates entirely within what Wilfrid Sellars has called the "space of reasons."[2] Beliefs about external objects are to be justified by an inference from beliefs about the effects these external objects produce in us. Our beliefs about the external world are confirmed when the complex of sensations, or sense-data, or impressions immediately evident might well be produced by the set of objects we are positing and we have available no reasonable alternative.

Just because it operates within the space of reasons, the traditional theory of perception is not equipped to tackle the fundamental problem of perception introduced in the beginning. I began by defining perception as "the process by which somehow or other we acquire beliefs about the external world on the basis of an input from that external world fed in through the senses." The fundamental problem of perception is to explain *how* we get from a sensory input described in physiological terms to the organized knowledge of the external world that we believe we possess, and on which we rely to conduct our affairs. We have seen how the traditional theory of perception has failed to solve this problem, but we can now see that the traditional theory *could not* solve this problem, because its key concept of inference does not allow us to connect our judgments of perception to their basis in the physical domain. Inference is an operation that connects judgments within the space of reasons. What we

---

2 "In characterizing an episode or a state as that [better, one] of *knowing*, we are not giving an empirical description of that episode or state, we are placing it in the logical space of reasons, of justifying and being able to justify what one says." Wilfrid A. Sellars, "Empiricism and the Philosophy of Mind," 298–9.

need is a way of connecting the judgments that form the domain of reasons to a basis in the physical world.

This notion of a space of reasons emphasizes the seriousness of the gap between the set of beliefs about the environment that are already in place and the physiological activity in the sensory system that we assume to be the basis for these beliefs. The traditional notion of sensation was introduced as the missing link to close this gap. On the one hand, the sensation is causally connected to the activity in the brain by which it is thrown up; on the other hand, the sensation is immediately available in consciousness to become an object of cognition. The sensation has a foot in both camps. It belongs to the causal system as an effect produced by physiological processes; it belongs to the cognitive system as an object available in consciousness.

We have already seen that the inferences invoked by the traditional theory to confirm or correct our commonsense beliefs about the world presuppose a set of beliefs about a causally organized system of physical objects that could not be acquired by such inferences. We now see that there is an equal problem of how we acquire the judgments regarding the character of the effects produced in our conscious experience, judgments which form the premises for our inferences to the external world. These two formidable problems constitute unfinished business, which I must face up to in due course. But we need not wait upon a solution to these problems to allow that the pattern of inference from sensation to external cause employed in the traditional theory is both legitimate and important.

Apart from the most determined sceptic, everyone accepts the general validity of our beliefs about a causally organized external world, which is presupposed in the traditional theory of perception. But not everyone may be prepared to concede the kind of knowledge of an inner domain of sensations, etc., which is required to provide the premises for the inferences in the traditional theory. The question for some may be not *how* it is possible to have an introspective knowledge of the inner world of consciousness, but *whether* such a knowledge is possible. This is one more hurdle to surmount before we can bring back the traditional theory, even in its new, less ambitious, form.

To make inferences to the external causes we must be able to begin by describing the sensations that are the effects. The possibility of describing such inner items, accessible only to the subject, has been challenged through an appeal to the private language argument associated with Ludwig Wittgenstein. This is a tricky and complicated issue, which I shall tackle in chapter 5. In the meantime, I shall point out merely that the defensive posture of the traditional theory has been immeasurably improved, now that the claim to explain the original acquisition of empirical beliefs has been given up. If the inferences from sensations involved in the causal representative theory take place only in a context in which our ordinary beliefs about the world are already in place, there is no need to provide a description of these sensations from a standing start. We can use in the description of immediate experience concepts derived from our encounter with the world. I can describe a certain patch in my visual field as kangaroo-shaped, because I know what kangaroos are and what they look like from various positions. I can then use the available evidence to decide whether the patch is produced by a real kangaroo or in some other way.

Other people will be able to understand the description I give of my experience, because kangaroos, we suppose, will normally produce similar visual sensations in similar observers. Other people know what it is like to experience a kangaroo-shaped patch, because they have also experienced such a patch when looking at a kangaroo. They are able to tell that this is the kind of experience I am having, because there is a word in our language through which I can refer to the cause of my sensation. Once the inference from sensations to their causes is no longer required to make possible our beliefs about the external world, an enormous burden has been lifted. We can introduce the pattern of inference at the heart of the traditional theory, with permission to assume our common-sense beliefs about our environment and the language in which we share these beliefs with our fellows.

The original function of this inferential pattern, as I suggested at the beginning of chapter 1, is to justify or correct beliefs about the world that are already on the table. Determining the character of the sensations produced in my experience, I make inferences to the external objects that are likely to be responsible. This is merely a special case of a general procedure by which I determine the true nature of an object by an inference from its effects on other things. Particularly important is the inspection of the effects that external objects have upon a specially constructed set of external things, called scientific instruments. I can determine the exact weight of an object by arranging an experiment in which it balances, precisely, a set of other things whose weight is already known. Although I can get a rough idea of the weight of a medium-sized object by holding it out in front of me, registering the feelings of stress I experience directly, the use of the balance gives more precision.

I am assuming that causal inferences of this kind are workable, but I have nothing special to say about *how* they work. This is the general philosophical problem of abduction about which a great deal has been written and my suspicion is that I would have nothing useful to add. My argument is that the general pattern is not radically altered in the special case where the effects involved are sensations produced in us.[3]

In saying that I may use inferences from my sensations to confirm or justify empirical beliefs, I am not suggesting that they provide *conclusive* confirmation or *final* justification. This would be a very controversial position, requiring defence. I am using the words "justify" and "confirm" in a much more low-key way, just as we may say that the story told by one witness is confirmed by what another has to say, even though it may turn out in the end that both are lying. The confirmation provided by the inference to the cause of my sensations may satisfy me, so that I now say that I know what is out there; but this does not mean that I have conclusive proof and am not prepared to re-open the matter.

The mistake of the traditional theory, then, is to use the structure of inference involved in this quite sophisticated second pass to explain the original acquisition of our primitive beliefs about the external world. This cannot be done, because the inferences involved in the second pass depend on assumptions about a causally connected system of physical objects that cannot be available in the initial stages of our cognitive life. Nevertheless, the second pass can provide a *justification in experience* for the empirical beliefs that are the outcome of the primitive perceptual process. I can justify my belief that there is a table in front of me, if I can identify sensations which are most likely produced by a table in that position.

Once we recognize that the pattern of inference used in the causal representative theory is available only on a second pass, so that it cannot reveal the structure of the system through which we originally acquire our empirical beliefs, it is not only much more defensible, but also much more innocuous. In principle, it can be used to check any belief, but it would normally confirm what we already know and would be a pointless waste of time. I can confirm my belief: "Here is a hand!," using the argument that I am presently enjoying the sort of visual sensation normally produced by light reflected from a human hand. In this kind of case, however, confirmation is not really required. There are certainly abnormal cases where the theory is useful. We can explain the afterimage which appears on the wall after looking away from a bright light: here we have a visual sensation not produced in the usual way by a change in the colour of the wall, but through some other, more complicated, causal process. In general, the theory seems to be most useful in explaining

3 In an earlier book, I do discuss, however, a complex pattern of causal inference used to move from regularities in experience to causal connections in the external world. See D.L.C. Maclachlan, *Philosophy of Perception*, 78–80.

and correcting cases of misperception, illusion, and hallucination. By paying close attention to the conditions of observation or the intermediate factors in the causal process, I can sometimes detect illusions and correct my original beliefs. This makes sense, since a focus on errors in perception has been a powerful reason for introducing the theory in the first place.

Thus, the operation that the classical account puts at the centre of its theory of knowledge *is* a perfectly legitimate procedure. It *is* possible to describe and classify our own sensations and experiences. It *is* possible to recognize that these experiences are produced by external factors in the environment. It *is* possible to make inferences from the character of our sensations to the things in the external world that produced them. What is *not* possible is to put this operation at the beginning of our quest for knowledge. On the contrary, this is a capacity we can only develop later – an inference from sensations to their causes is possible only when we have already constructed a world governed by causal laws. The main reason why this system develops, albeit at a later point in our intellectual development, is to explain and correct the errors in instinctive judgments about the environment when they have proved unsatisfactory.

3 THE METHOD OF ANALYTIC INTROSPECTION

The success of this technique in particular cases suggested to some philosophers and psychologists the possibility of a comprehensive review of the entire corpus of our empirical beliefs. Perhaps we can provide a philosophical *reconstruction* of our empirical knowledge, beginning with a clear delineation of the given sensations produced in us by external causes and proceeding by sound causal reasoning to a set of secure judgments about the real nature of the external world. This program has its attractions, since it merely extends and generalizes a procedure that has been used successfully to explain and handle particular errors and illusions.

This, at any rate, was the project adopted around the beginning of the twentieth century by a group of psychologists such as E.B. Titchener,[4] who called this method "Analytic Introspection." The method did not, however, enjoy the anticipated success, partly because it proved difficult to provide a secure articulation and description of the sensations that were to serve as the basis for the construction of empirical knowledge. For one thing, it was hard to provide an informative characterization of immediate experience without using ideas drawn from our knowledge of

4 See *An Outline of Psychology.*

the external world. As I explained in the preceding section, I can describe a specific image in the visual field as "kangaroo-shaped," because it is similar to the visual images normally produced by real kangaroos. This is fair enough, if I am explaining how I have been fooled by a kangaroo cardboard cutout. But it is circular if I am trying to provide a neutral description of immediate experience, which will be a basis for the construction of an objective world which includes kangaroos. Things actually work the other way round. The notion of "kangaroo-shaped" is derivative from the concept of kangaroo I apply to certain animals found in Australia. I begin by forming concepts of various kinds of animals, perhaps because of a primitive concern to distinguish animals I can eat from animals that can eat me!

The assumptions and concepts which are legitimate and necessary in the piecemeal inferences used in ordinary life from experiences to objects must, however, be strictly disallowed in the systematic program of analytic introspection devised by Titchener. The disciplined introspection practiced by followers of Titchener was designed to guard against what Titchener called the "stimulus error."[5] This error was introduced when one began to think about the external stimulus producing the sensation, rather than concentrating on the raw sensation experienced. These restrictions made introspection all the more difficult and it proved impossible to get useful and consistent results.[6]

Even if the first hurdle had been successfully overcome with the compilation of a vast store of data revealed through introspection, there would still be the fearsome problem of collecting the evidence to establish the causal correlations necessary to justify inferences from sensations to external objects. Thus, it was not surprising that the results achieved by this method turned out to be so disappointing. It was not, however, illegitimate in principle, provided that it is borne in mind that what was attempted was a philosophical *reconstruction* of empirical knowledge, and not an *explanation* of how the original empirical beliefs were formed in response to the sensory input. If there is confusion on this point, the collapse of the reconstruction would require us to recognize that our primary empirical beliefs lack a proper explanation, so that scepticism would be given a foothold. But the very introduction of the sensations as the effects of external causes affecting the senses presupposes a generally valid system of beliefs about the external world. The

---

5 E.B. Titchener, "The Schema of Introspection," 488.

6 The authority of introspection was also seriously weakened by a disagreement among senior researchers about the existence of imageless thought. See *Stanford Encyclopedia of Philosophy*, "Mental Imagery," 3.2.

reconstruction of empirical knowledge cannot even be undertaken as a project, unless our original beliefs about our environment are by and large taken for granted.

With this breakdown in the method of analytic introspection, designed to capture the essence of the elements of immediate experience as they are in themselves, it would appear that the philosophical importance of the pattern of inference involved in the traditional theory has largely evaporated. There is no longer any prospect for the reconstruction of our knowledge of the physical world, based on an exact delineation of the experiences that world has formed within us. What we are left with is no more than a piecemeal strategy for fixing mistakes in perceptual beliefs through inferences from the sensations produced in us, taking account of the distortions caused by the conditions of observation. The conceptual scheme of the traditional theory makes it possible for us to make sense of illusions such as afterimages and Macbeth's dagger.

3

Primary and Secondary Qualities

1 INTRODUCTION

The downgrading of the traditional theory of perception at the end of the last chapter overlooks, however, a really major innovation associated with it. At the beginning of the seventeenth century a certain scientific picture of the world became dominant. This was the conception of the physical world as essentially matter in motion. Material objects had no more than certain special primary qualities, such as size, shape, motion, and number, which could be handled mathematically by the new science. What will happen, then, to the other properties we normally assign to physical things, such as tastes, smells, and colours? The belief that physical objects really have the smells and colours we directly experience must be a mistake.

A massive and systematic error on this scale is perhaps too big to be called a mistake, but the point is that the discrepancy between what we normally think and what the scientist declares to be the case can be handled by the same theory used to explain the familiar discrepancies – between what we experience and what is actually there – associated with illusions and hallucinations. The key distinction is between the sensations produced in us and their external causes. The colours and smells directly experienced are merely sensations produced in us, from which we must infer the causes which produced them. We may naively assume that the experienced sensations *replicate* properties of the external objects, but the system will work and provide information about the external world so long as the sensations *correspond* with properties of the external things. The great advantage of the change from replication to correspondence is that it allows the positing of the real world described in the new science. Corresponding to different sensations in the mind are different arrangements of the matter in motion in the world.

Therefore, the commonsense belief that the real world actually contains the colours, smells, and sounds that we directly experience, is mistaken. But even this massive systematic error can be handled by our normal procedures for correcting mistakes through focusing on the sensations produced in us and then making the best inference to the true cause.

2 DESCARTES

What cannot work, of course, is to take what is essentially a system for correcting mistakes on a second pass and turn it into the primary basis for empirical knowledge. This is precisely what Descartes attempted through the use of his celebrated Method of Doubt. Since knowledge acquired through the senses is unreliable (perhaps it would be fairer to say "not completely reliable"), he argues that it must be swept aside and a new basis sought in the ideas immediately present in the mind. Relying on proofs of the existence of God, who could be invoked to validate the innate ideas and principles required, Descartes believed that he could get us back the external physical world. What we get back, however, is not the vibrant world of common sense he has thrown out, but an austere world of matter in motion, conforming to the categories of the new science. It is clear that to replace the familiar world of common sense in the interests of the new science is the ulterior motive (the subtext) of the whole enterprise. Whatever his motives, Descartes' strategy for reinstating the physical world depends on his proofs of the existence of God, which are not widely accepted today[1] and are certainly more open to doubt than the commonsense beliefs that fall at the hands of Descartes' "very powerful Deceiver." It must therefore be conceded that the Cartesian attempt to derive the existence of the external world from ideas in the mind, relying on innate principles certified by God, is a failure.

3 JOHN LOCKE

Although the empiricism of John Locke does not permit him the innate ideas and principles assumed by Descartes, he concurs with Descartes in the use of the "way of ideas" to explain the replacement of the commonsense view of the external world by the picture provided by the new science. Although Locke does not appear to register that in attacking innate principles, certified by God, he is ruling out our one hope of

---

1 One common complaint is that the proofs are circular, depending on principles that God must be invoked to validate.

basing empirical knowledge on an argument from ideas in the mind to things in the external world, he firmly commits himself to the standard theory of the day, which he shares with the Cartesians, that in perception the immediate object is the idea of sensation.

Locke required this doctrine to operate the celebrated distinction between primary and secondary qualities, which was central to the new science. This distinction was not, of course, introduced by Locke; it was widely accepted among the advocates of the new science, such as Galileo, Gassendi, Descartes, and Thomas Hobbes, although they did not use the special terms "primary qualities" and "secondary qualities," which were due to Sir Robert Boyle.[2] For Boyle, indeed, the secondary qualities were the colours, smells, and tastes directly experienced; for Locke, when he was being careful, such items were *ideas* of secondary qualities. The secondary qualities represented by these ideas "are nothing in the objects themselves, but powers to produce various sensations in us by their primary qualities."[3] These primary qualities, in turn, are represented in the mind through *ideas of primary qualities*.[4]

4 THE QUESTION OF COLOUR

To clarify the theory advocated by John Locke it may help to focus on a special case. I have chosen the question of colour, which has received the widest discussion. We naively believe that the colours we experience exist independently and continue to exist when they are no longer perceived. We soon find out, however, that matters are not that simple.

If I put on special glasses that filter the light coming to my eyes, it will appear to me that the things in the world have all changed colour. This is a mistake that can be easily explained by saying that the colours I experience after putting on the glasses are nothing but effects produced in my experience by light coming from the objects and filtered by the special glasses. It is a mistake to attribute these colours to the objects involved. But is it not equally true that the colours I experience without the glasses are nothing but effects produced in me by light reflected from the objects? Will it not be equally a mistake to attribute the perceived colours to the objects in the world in the way we do? Must we not recognize that the colours directly experienced are not properties of external

2 See Richard I. Aaron, *John Locke*, 120–3.

3 John Locke, *An Essay Concerning Human Understanding*, II. viii. 10.

4 Locke, incidentally, introduces a third class of qualities which are the powers of the objects to produce changes in other things. He instances "the power in fire to produce a new colour, or consistency, in *wax* or *clay*." *Essay*, II. viii. 10.

objects and have no being without the mind? It will be a serious matter if we have to deny that the things in the world are coloured, that roses are red and lemons are yellow. We will no longer be able to distinguish different kinds of things through their different colours: we will no longer be able to distinguish a ripe lemon, which is yellow, from an unripe lemon, which is green. Moreover, the ingenious and growing system of colour coding will have to be shut down.

The solution is, of course, that the revelation introduced through conceiving our sense experiences as effects of external stimuli must be accompanied by a paradigm shift in what it means to say that the objects in the world are variously red, green, blue, etc. The vulgar, as Hume would put it, believe that a rose is red, if and only if it has as its property the red colour we immediately experience. The learned change the criterion so that a rose is red if and only if it has the *power* to generate, in suitable circumstances, the appropriate sensations in the perceiving subject. This was the move made by John Locke himself through his distinction between secondary qualities and their corresponding ideas. This maneuver allows us to salvage a whole area of discourse, retaining the customary distinctions between what is true and what is false. It remains true that grass is green and false that grass is red.

We assign the colours we do to the things around us in virtue of the kinds of sensations they produce in us in *standard* circumstances. This way of explaining our procedure is designed to conform to the traditional causal representative theory, but the procedure itself is certainly used in ordinary life to deal with certain anomalies. To be able to identify them, we want to have physical objects that retain their colour properties in the face of the vagaries of the light. In a special light a red rose may *look* a different colour, but it still remains a red rose. In assessing the true colours of things, we disallow what is experienced in nonstandard conditions.

We must now move down to a third level. The disposition to produce specific sensations of colour in certain circumstances must itself depend on some character of the surface from which the light is reflected, which we may call its pigmentation. This character of the surface will be an objective character, in no way linked to the perceptions of human beings. These objective colour properties of grass and other things can be established without involving our visual systems. Scientific instruments will establish differences in surface pigmentation by recording which wavelengths of light falling on the surface are absorbed and which are reflected.

The three levels which I have distinguished – ideas of sensation in the mind, powers in the objects to produce these ideas (secondary qualities),

primary qualities on which these powers depend – were clearly distinguished by John Locke.[5] What Locke did not have available was a way
of clearly articulating the categorical basis on which the dispositional
colour properties or powers of the object depend, since the electromagnetic theory this requires was not developed until the nineteenth century. A contemporary version of Locke's theory can thus provide a much
more solid and complete account than was possible for Locke himself.

If there were an exact match between the range of pigments distinguished through scientific instruments and the range of pigments we
accept through the exercise of our visual faculties, we could provide a
quick solution to the vexed question of the objectivity of colour. The
colours that appear in immediate experience are subjective and depend
upon the special character of our perceptual apparatus, whereas the
colour differences we assign to external objects would be quite objective. Unfortunately, things are not as simple as this. We know that there
are people who are red/green colour blind, and who cannot detect differences in the pigmentation of surfaces, confirmed by the scientific
instruments, which are available to the rest of us. There are other real
differences in pigmentation which no one is equipped to detect.

The fact is that the sensations of colour we experience can be produced in a variety of different ways. This fact has facilitated colour repro-
duction and has permitted the development of simple systems of colour
television. All the colours we see can be produced by a suitable combination of emissions from just three phosphors, so that the visual representation we experience when looking at the television screen simulates so
successfully the representation we would get by looking at the collection
of objects depicted. The person on television *looks* like the person in real
life, because the visual sensation associated with television *is* like the visual sensation in real life! This has been carefully contrived, although
the packet of light waves coming to the eye from the television screen is
very different from the complex of light waves that would have entered
the eye with the direct observation of the scene depicted.

It follows from all this that our visual system has a limited capacity to
detect differences in the objective character of the surfaces from which
the light has been reflected. What should we say, then, when we get the
same sensation of colour from light reflected by two objects, where the
reflected light has a significantly different spectral power distribution?[6]
Are the two surfaces the same or different colours? If we say that the

---

5 *An Essay Concerning Human Understanding*, II. viii.

6 The spectral power distribution of a light signal is specified by how much energy the
light contains at every wavelength in the visible spectrum.

surfaces are both green because of the kind of sensation that they are accustomed to produce in the observer, then we will have to concede that the colours of objects are not defined in a completely objective fashion, but only relative to the experiences of a special class of observer. Presumably, other animals with different visual systems might want to attribute a quite different range of colours to the objects they encounter;[7] they *must* do this if they are sensitive to colours in the ultraviolet range!

If we wish to provide a truly objective description of the "colour" properties of the surfaces from which light is reflected, we cannot use our ordinary colour vocabulary at all. We have to specify which wavelengths of visible light are absorbed by the surface of the object and which wavelengths are reflected. Such a description would be quite independent of the visual capacities of any observer. This determination of the colour of the object does depend, however, on the use of elaborate instrumentation that we do not carry around with us. For practical purposes – such as distinguishing ripe and unripe lemons – we have to use our ordinary classifications, which depend on the powers of the object to produce in us certain kinds of visual sensations. Although these classifications certainly involve a subjective element, they are not entirely subjective, insofar as these powers of the object do depend on the real pigmentation of the surface as determined scientifically. What *is* subjective is the *grouping* of different varieties of pigmentation, in virtue of having the same power to produce the same kind of colour in immediate experience.

The colour words we use to group surfaces into the same class can actually be shown to be relative, not just to human visual equipment, but also to the social and linguistic group to which we belong. Prime Minister Gladstone, aware of the difficulties of translating colour words from Homeric Greek into English, thought that the Greeks of the time of Homer had more primitive capacities for colour discrimination![8] It is now recognized that the lack of strict equivalences between colour words in certain languages (such as English and Gaelic) are the result of different ways of carving up the continuum of colour experienced. This is a second level of non-objectivity, but again we have different groupings for what has an objective basis in the real world.

In this discussion I have been focusing on the colour properties of surfaces and of the objects to which these surfaces belong. It is important to

---

7 It is said that bulls are not enraged by red rags because they are colour blind, although I am not sure that I would want to test this theory in the field!

8 "The organ of colour and its impressions were but partially developed among the Greeks of the heroic age." William Ewart Gladstone. Quoted in the entry on colour categorization, *The MIT Encyclopedia of the Cognitive Sciences*, 143.

note, however, that colour is also assigned to the quality of the light emitted by a source. Indeed, the colour of light may be said to be more fundamental, insofar as the colour of a surface depends on the colour of the
light reflected from it. The account of the colour of light will conform
closely to the account already given for the colour of surfaces. Again, we
must distinguish between the objective colour composition of the light
(its spectral power distribution), which is to be determined scientifically
with the aid of a spectrograph, and the colour we assign to the light in
ordinary life, which depends on the kind of sensation it is accustomed to
generate. Because the quality of the light determines the kind of sensation, there is normally a good fit between the colour we assign to the light
and its composition as determined objectively, but there are cases where
we describe lights as the same colour without there being a close affinity
in their objective composition.

To sum up, we find in Locke's account three levels at which colours
may be distinguished. First, we discern differences in colour presented
in immediate experience: these colours Locke calls "ideas of secondary
qualities." Second, corresponding to these ideas are the secondary qualities, which are nothing but powers in the object to produce certain ideas
of colour in the consciousness of the observer in certain specific circumstances. Since these powers in the object produce their typical effects *in
standard circumstances* the way is open for a thing whose real colour (secondary quality) does not change to produce different experiences in a
variety of circumstances. For example, a white face may look pink in a
red-light district. It is also true that the same colour experience, e.g.
pink, may be brought about in different conditions by objects of a different colour. We classify the real colours of objects in terms of how they
look in standard circumstances.

At the third level, we must assign to the secondary qualities, which are
dispositional properties, a categorical basis in the nature of things.
According to Locke, secondary qualities "are nothing in the objects
themselves but powers to produce various sensations in us by their primary qualities, i.e. by the bulk, figure, texture, and motion of their in-
sensible parts."[9] Although specific powers or dispositional properties
must have *some* basis in the primary qualities of the object, it does not
follow that the same dispositional property is necessarily grounded in
the same collection of primary qualities. It is known that different kinds
of light may produce the same experience of colour in persons with
normal vision. We might not want to say that these different kinds of

9 *An Essay Concerning Human Understanding*, II. viii. 10.

light are lights of a different colour, but if we do, we have a third level at which colours may be different.

5 INVERTED QUALIA

We have seen that the same colour sensations may be produced in us by light of different wavelengths; it is also possible for different sensations of colour to be produced in different people by light of the same wavelength. Because of the phenomenon of colour blindness, it is clear that not everyone experiences colours in exactly the same way. There are people unlike the rest of us who cannot distinguish red and green. It follows that when such people look at red and green traffic lights, they cannot be having the same colour experiences as everyone else. These differences have led philosophers to speculate about other differences between people who distinguish precisely the same range of colours in the physical world. I look at grass and call it green and I look at the sky and call it blue; you look at grass and call it green and you look at the sky and call it blue. But how do I know that you are experiencing the same green and blue that I do? Perhaps when you look at the sky you experience the same colour that I experience when I look at grass, and when you look at grass you experience the same colour that I do when I look at the sky! The technical name for such bizarre contingencies is "inverted qualia."[10]

This idea was introduced many years ago by John Locke in his *Essay Concerning Human Understanding*:

Though one Man's Idea of Blue should be different from another's. Neither would it carry any imputation of falsehood to our simple ideas, if by the different structure of our organs it were so ordered that *the same object should produce in several men's minds different ideas* at the same time; v.g. if the idea that a violet produced in one man's mind by his eyes were the same that a marigold produced in another man's and *vice versa*. For, since this could never be known, because one man's mind could not pass into another man's body, to perceive what appearances were produced by those organs, neither the idea hereby, nor the names would be at all confounded, or any falsehood be in either. For all things that had the texture of a violet producing constantly the idea which he called blue, and those which had the texture of a marigold producing constantly the idea which he called yellow, whatever those appearances were in his mind, he would be able

10 See, for instance, David Chalmers, *The Conscious Mind*, chapter 7, section 4, where, indeed, the quotation from Locke which I give is to be found.

as regularly to distinguish things for his use by those appearances, and understand and signify those distinctions marked by the names "blue" and "yellow," as if the appearances or ideas in his mind received from those two flowers were exactly the same with the ideas in other men's minds.[11] (Book 2, chapter 32, section 15)

The point is that although people could not operate in the way they do with their concept of yellow apart from what may be called the "stuffing" provided through visual sensation, different people can be employing what is in a sense the same concept of yellow to discriminate the same range of coloured objects, even if the visual sensations involved are radically different. Of course, the natural assumption is that this is not the case: I naturally believe that everyone else has the same range of colour experiences correlated with sensory input as I do. Thus, I naturally believe that I can communicate to my fellows, not only the colour properties of external objects, but also the character of my private experiences, since I naturally believe that in similar circumstances other people have the same sort of experiences as I do myself. Philosophical reflection discloses the slightly worrying possibility that I may be wrong about this, and if I am, the language in which I try to describe to you my various sensations will not convey what I actually experience. If my experiences are of a completely unique character, then the language I use to describe them will not convey what I actually experience – it will be a private language not correctly understood by anyone else.[12] But if my experiences are not unique in this way, as seems reasonable given our common heredity and similar biological make-up, then other people will understand exactly what I mean when I say that I am experiencing yellow or feeling pain.

For the sake of completeness, I should point out that it is possible for me to operate with some sort of concept of yellow – albeit a "gutted" concept of yellow – without ever experiencing the appropriate sensation. I could learn to use the word "yellow," applying it to the same range of objects as other people, if necessary by using a meter that registered the character of the light reflected from surfaces. I would not, indeed, have the full concept of yellow, complete with stuffing, but if I were discreet in the use of my meter, no one would detect my handicap! I may lack the sensation either because the limited number of objects that produce this

11 *An Essay Concerning Human Understanding*, II. xxxii. 15
12 Such a private language will not, indeed, be a *logically* private language, in the sense to be explained in chapter 5, section 3.

sensation have never come within my ken,[13] or because the peculiar wiring of my visual system does not generate the distinctive experience.

A fascinating example of this has recently been uncovered by Oliver Sacks and set out in an article in *The New Yorker*. The example, indeed, concerns stereoscopic vision rather than colour perception, but the principle is the same. Sue Barry was born cross-eyed, and although operations were performed to correct this, they were done too late to permit the development of stereoscopic vision. She was not unduly handicapped, being able to judge distance in other ways, and she did not realize what she was lacking until she took a course in neurophysiology in college. When she talked to Oliver Sacks in 1996, she even thought that she could imagine what it was like to have stereoscopic vision, having become a professor of neurophysiology and having read everything available on the topic. In 2004 she wrote again and said that she had been wrong. In the interim, through strenuous efforts and professional help, she had actually developed the stereoscopic vision she had been missing all her life and it had been a complete revelation! She now knew what it was like to enjoy the kind of visual experience which most of us take for granted, and it was something she could not have anticipated even with all her scientific knowledge.[14]

13 This is like Mary, the brain scientist (invented by Frank Jackson), who has always been confined in a black and white environment and never seen colours. My point is actually more simple-minded and my person does not have to be a brain scientist. See Frank Jackson, "Epiphenomenal Qualia," 127–36.

14 Oliver Sacks, "Stereo Sue," *The New Yorker*, 19 June 2006, 64–73.

4

Primary Qualities and the Physical World

1 THE ATTACK ON LOCKE'S DISTINCTION
BY BARRY STROUD

Locke's distinction between the ideas of primary qualities and the ideas of secondary qualities is a fundamental component in his theory, but it has been a source of trouble for a very long time, at least since the time of Bishop Berkeley.[1] The primary qualities are those qualities that characterize the things that really exist in the physical world, and upon which the various powers of these objects depend. The secondary qualities are nothing but the powers of the objects to produce in us sensations of colour, taste, smell, etc.

If we work with the framework, which explains visual perception in terms of sensations produced in the mind by external causes, it is clear that the apparent colour and shape and size are closely integrated in our visual experience. When we look at a tomato, we are presented with a red, bulgy patch and the red colour is experienced as spread out over a specific area of the visual field. Moreover, just as the apparent colour varies with the conditions of observation, so also does the apparent shape and size. Things look smaller as they get further away. From the top of a tall building, people on the ground look like ants. There is also a change in how the top surface of a table will look when we change the angle from which it is viewed. How, then, can we imagine a fundamental difference between the colour and the extension of the coloured patches that we are getting in experience?

Locke can easily concede that the colours and shapes immediately experienced are closely integrated and vary equally with the conditions of

---

1 A systematic attack on the distinction is to be found in the first of *Three Dialogues between Hylas and Philonous*.

observation, since these items have the same standing as ideas in the mind. What he distinguishes are the qualities of things that correspond to these ideas. This is why experienced colours are said to be ideas of secondary qualities and experienced shapes are said to be ideas of primary qualities.

In his recent book *The Quest for Reality* Barry Stroud attempts to overturn Locke's distinction. Stroud begins by explaining colour properties in much the same way as Locke himself. Basically, the property of yellowness is the power or dispositional property of the object to produce perceptions of yellow in the perceiver. This simple account must be modified in order to allow yellow things to remain yellow in a variety of circumstances, e.g. when there is a change in the light. Stroud gives the following analysis of the colour "yellow" as ascribed to some physical thing x: "x is yellow if and only if normal human perceivers standing in certain relations R to x in certain kinds of perceptual circumstances C would get perceptions of yellow." He recognizes, of course, that "'normal human perceivers' would have to be explained, and the relations of orientation R and the surrounding conditions C would have to be specified concretely" (121). He calls the fully specified version of the statement "the bi-conditional about yellow things" and believes that it is true.

Stroud's strategy is to construct a corresponding bi-conditional about rectangular things: "x is rectangular, if and only if normal human perceivers standing in certain relations R to x in certain kinds of perceptual circumstances C would get perceptions of rectangularity." In both cases we have a property of the object introduced on the left hand side of the bi-conditional that is connected to a dispositional property introduced on the right hand side. We can certainly think of the typical range of sensations that rectangular objects produce in us in various circumstances. This allows Stroud to insert a dispositional property of rectangularity, although it would be difficult, perhaps impossible, to fully specify the dispositional property without assuming an objective property of rectangularity determined, for instance, by careful measurement. In any event, our standard idea of the rectangular remains an idea of a primary quality, to which the dispositional property, if we insist on introducing it, would be merely contingently related. In other possible worlds, *different* dispositional properties might be associated with rectangularity. The idea is that rectangular things would be just as rectangular as they are even if they did not produce the kind of representations they do in human perceivers, whereas yellow things could not remain yellow if they did not in normal circumstances generate sensations of yellow in the typical perceiving subject.

To protect the distinction between primary and secondary qualities against the arrival of the bi-conditional about rectangular things, it is essential to maintain that the bi-conditional about yellow things is a noncontingent analysis of "x is yellow" or, in the older terminology of Locke, that "yellow" is a secondary quality that is nothing but a power. Stroud attacks this position by imagining a world in which yellow and blue things changed places, so that "perceivers normally got only perceptions of blue from those yellow lemons, and perceptions of yellow only from objects that are blue" (128). Presumably, Stroud is imagining a change in our visual equipment, so that what are now yellow things will produce the sensations formerly produced by things that are blue.

Certainly, in the changed world Stroud posits, the things that now produce sensations of yellow would produce sensations of blue. The crucial question, however, is whether the things we now call yellow would still be yellow in such a world. If they remain yellow, which is the claim made by Stroud, there will be no more than a contingent connection between the colour of the object and the kind of sensation produced in the mind, which will wipe out the supposed distinction in status between yellowness and rectangularity.

The answer to the crucial question depends, however, on what we mean by "yellow." Locke clearly distinguishes between the secondary qualities, which are nothing but powers, and the intrinsic properties of the objects on which these powers depend. Does the word "yellow" refer to a dispositional property or to the categorical basis on which it depends? There is a change in the dispositional properties of yellow things in the world imagined by Stroud. Things that now have a disposition to produce sensations of yellow will have a disposition to produce sensations of blue. On the other hand, there will be no change in the categorical basis. Every disposition necessarily rests on a categorical basis, which does not change with every change we imagine in the disposition. The disposition of a lemon to produce sensations of yellow will change in a world in which lemons produce sensations of blue in normal perceivers. But the categorical basis in the lemon that generates these different sensations in these different worlds will not change.

In Stroud's biconditional, does the expression on the left hand side "x is yellow" designate a dispositional property of x? In this case, the biconditional will be the definition of a type of dispositional property and noncontingent and the lemon will no longer be yellow in the other world. Or does the expression "x is yellow" designate the categorical basis of the dispositional property? In this case, the biconditional will be contingent and the lemon will remain yellow.

We can certainly make a case that the normal use of colour words is to refer to dispositional properties of the objects concerned. We group things together as the same colour in virtue of their power to produce the same sensations in normal circumstances. We discovered in the last chapter (section 4) that the same dispositional property does not always have the same categorical basis, since the same sensations can be produced in various ways.

Suppose, however, Stroud insists that there is a sense of "yellow" that does denote the categorical basis. He might want to define a pure yellow light as a light of *a certain definite wavelength*,[2] and refuse to change his definition whatever changes might take place in the visual sensations typically produced by this kind of light in some other possible world. Then he would have his contingent connection between pure yellow light and the associated dispositional properties in the different worlds. But the term "pure yellow light" is referring to the categorical basis on which the secondary quality depends, which according to Locke is described through an idea of *primary* quality. This special, scientific sense of "yellow light" is defined as light of a certain specific wavelength, and the idea of the length of waves is, of course, for Locke an idea of primary quality!

The upshot of this discussion is that what is special about primary qualities is not that they are a special kind of dispositional property but that they constitute the categorical basis on which all dispositional properties depend. The ideas of primary qualities are special, not because they are seen to have a special status in immediate experience, but because they are those aspects of sensation that we use to capture the true character of external objects. The distinguishing of ideas of primary qualities is therefore associated with the project of the new science to describe the true nature of the external reality. This project will be discussed in the next section.

2 THE NATURE OF THE PHYSICAL WORLD

At the beginning of his book The Nature of the Physical World,[3] Sir Arthur Eddington distinguishes between two tables – the table of common sense and the scientific table. For Eddington there are duplicates of every object about him, including the table at which he sits down to write. One of these tables has been familiar from earliest years. "It is a commonplace object of that environment I call the world ... It has extension; it is comparatively permanent; it is coloured; above all, it is substantial" (5). The second table is the scientific table, which is mostly

2 I call this pure yellow light, because there are combinations of light of different wavelengths that also produce sensations of yellow.

3 Sir Arthur Eddington, *The Nature of the Physical World*, 5–12.

emptiness. "Sparsely scattered in that emptiness are numerous electric charges rushing about with great speed; but their combined bulk amounts to less than a billionth of the bulk of the table itself. Notwithstanding its strange construction, it turns out to be an entirely efficient table. It supports my writing paper ... for when I lay the paper on it the little electric particles with their headlong speed keep on hitting the underside, so that the paper is maintained in shuttlecock fashion at a nearly steady level" (6).

Of course, no one believes that there are really two tables, not even Eddington himself. One of the advantages of the traditional theory of perception is that it can clearly explain the replacement of the common-sense picture of the physical world with the picture developed in modern science. With the introduction of the second pass, we can re-open the question of what is truly responsible for the sensations produced in us. We originally imagine that our sensations are produced by a solid physical object with a certain size and shape, with a surface of a brownish colour. But we are now permitted to introduce other hypotheses about the external cause. Eddington posits "numerous electric charges rushing about at great speed," in accordance with the physics of the day. There is, of course, nothing final about this hypothesis and we may wish to move to a universe of very short two-dimensional strings vibrating in exotic dimensions.[4] We may move to whatever account theoretical physics introduces as the best possible hypothesis, so long as it "saves the appearances" and explains the sensations we get in our career as observers.

John Locke, of course, knew nothing about strings and electrostatic charges, but he did adopt an account of physical nature that was a more primitive version of these more up to date theories. Locke himself favoured the *corpuscular* theory supported by his friend Sir Robert Boyle, according to which our sensations are produced not by solid physical objects but by swarms of corpuscles. These corpuscles may be roughly equated with the molecules of modern chemistry. We can easily think of our visual sensations as produced by light reflected from swarms of molecules, instead of solid physical objects. The molecular theory has the advantage of providing a convincing explanation of the transformation of matter from gas to liquid, to liquid crystal, to crystal, as things cool down.

The list of primary qualities provided by Locke turns out to include precisely those qualities required to describe the corpuscles introduced in Boyle's theory. This is no coincidence. The original or primary

---

4 For a brief explanation of string theory, see Barry Dainton, *Time and Space*, chapter 20.

qualities of body are solidity, extension, figure, motion or rest, and number.[5] These qualities "the mind finds inseparable from every particle of matter, though less than to make itself singly be perceived by our senses."[6] What Locke has done is to pick out those features of the ideas given in sensation required to describe the corpuscles which constitute the real physical world, leaving the rest aside.

To confine ourselves to the sense of sight, the visual field that organizes our visual ideas contains items with some sort of size and shape and position in the field, items that may or may not change position or move. We are also able to provide a rough and ready count of similar items appearing at a certain time. It may be true that we largely use differences in colour to distinguish items in the visual field, but we may nevertheless drop concepts of colour from the list of abstract general ideas that we use to conceive the nature of the physical world. Size, shape, position, motion or rest, solidity, and number are all we require to operate the corpuscular theory.

We may say that a lemon (or the corpuscles that compose it) has the disposition to produce specific perceptions of shape and size in the perceiver; but the categorical basis of this disposition must be conceived as the real shape and size of the lemon described in objective geometrical terms. Unless we assume a real size and shape for the lemon, we cannot position the lemon in the world in such a way as to explain how the lemon can produce in the perceiver the sensations it does, and there would be no possibility of the second pass, involving the connection between objects and sensations, through which the learned come to believe that the perceived colours do not exist in the external world. Thus, the thesis that shape, size, position, etc. are primary qualities that are objectively real is a necessary condition of even formulating the theory that colours, tastes, and so on are secondary qualities with a different status.

3 SENSITIVE KNOWLEDGE

The list of primary qualities provided by Locke is hard to dispute, so long as we accept the corpuscular theory of physical nature. This grand unified theory will include perforce a corpuscular theory of light, interpreting the light rays responsible for our visual sensations as a stream of corpuscles traveling from the object to the eye. Such a theory was in fact defended by Sir Isaac Newton, and most other scientists of the time. Any

5 This is the list Locke gives in *An Essay Concerning Human Understanding*, II. viii. 9.
6 Ibid.

improvements in Locke's list will come from advances in science that replace the corpuscular theory with more sophisticated notions. The major paradigm shift took place when the corpuscular theory of light was replaced by the wave theory, introducing concepts such as frequency and amplitude, and regulating this system of electromagnetic waves through the equations formulated by J.J. Maxwell. Once we get the idea of interpreting physical reality as the cause responsible for our sensations, we are permitted to describe that reality in whatever terms it takes to explain the functioning of the universe.

Even though the corpuscles introduced in Locke's theory were individually too small to see, we could imagine what they would look like with a suitable magnification and we could use certain aspects of our immediate sensations (ideas of primary qualities) to conceive their character. Nowadays, we feel that we have much less of a grip on what is really out there. We get less help from our immediate sensations, and the theories of the physicists are largely constituted by complex mathematics that most people cannot follow. Our ideas of the primary qualities of the ultimate constituents of matter have become less secure.

There is, however, a more fundamental objection to Locke's theory than the emendation of his list of primary qualities required by advances in science. This is the difficulty I identified in the second section of the first chapter as the Achilles' heel of the traditional theory of perception. If all that we can access in immediate experience is a set of ideas in the mind, what right do we have to assume that there are objects in an external world that produce some of these ideas and correspond to the ideas they produce?

Locke shows that he is aware of the problem in the *Essay*, when he writes: "How shall the mind, when it perceives nothing but its own ideas, know that they agree with things themselves?" (IV.iv.3). Although he concedes that this "seems not to want difficulty," he fails to appreciate how serious the problem is. The answer he gives in the next section is far from satisfactory. He argues that since we do not form simple ideas by putting together other ideas, these ideas "must necessarily be the product of things operating on the mind, in a natural way, and producing therein those perceptions which by the wisdom and will of our Maker they are ordained and adapted to" (IV.iv.4). This certainly does not follow, quite apart from the appeal to God reminiscent of the Cartesian argument: "There is a God and He is no Deceiver." Even if we accept simple ideas not formed by combining other ideas through an act of imagination, it does not follow that these simple ideas must have a source outside us.

I rescued the traditional pattern of inference from sensations to their external causes by turning it into a second pass, designed to confirm or correct beliefs about the external world originally acquired in some other way. There is no evidence that Locke avails himself of this strategy. He does, indeed, talk about *sensitive knowledge* which is "perceiving the existence of particular things" (IV.iv.3); but there is no reason to think that this is a revision of his standard view, according to which "It is evident the mind knows not things immediately, but only by the intervention of the ideas it has of them" (IV.iv.4).

The trouble with positing another way of acquiring knowledge about the world that does not involve an inference from sensations is that one may be reasonably asked to explain how this other route to knowledge is possible. This cannot be an absolute demand, since it is not a contradiction to accept some other route to empirical knowledge, while confessing that one can give no account of how this works. One can always fall back on the formula: "Somehow, I know not how," just as Locke, baffled in his attempt to explain the nature of substance, calls it "Something, I know not what." Nevertheless, it is not very satisfactory to leave things up in the air like that, and I shall devote the second part of this book to an attempt to deal with this issue.

Before I embark on this project I want to get another difficulty out of the way. The inference from sensations to their external causes depends on our capacity to determine the nature of the sensations that provide the basis for the inference. Until recent years this was not an issue that was even considered. There was no problem about distinguishing and describing the ideas of sensation that appear in immediate consciousness; the trick was to get beyond these ideas to a knowledge of the external world. With the introduction, by Ludwig Wittgenstein, of the private language argument, our knowledge of our own sensations could no longer be taken for granted. This is an argument I must answer if I am to defend the operation of the pattern of inference in the traditional theory, even as a second pass. Because of the complexities of the issue and the extensive discussion it has received in recent years, there is no short answer to the private language argument and the topic must be given a chapter to itself.

5

The Private Language Argument

1 RUSSELL'S NOMINALISM

Wittgenstein's private language argument was originally introduced to counter a theory, developed by Bertrand Russell, which combined a certain logical doctrine with a sense-datum epistemology. The logical doctrine was designed to provide the values for the individual variables introduced in the predicate calculus of *Principia Mathematica*. This was the theory of singular thoughts and logically proper names. Singular thoughts were thoughts whose essence was the introduction of an individual object; they were what would be described in Kantian terms as the intuitions of particulars. If the object did not exist, then neither did the associated singular thoughts. Moving to the domain of symbols, it was possible in virtue of such singular thoughts to bestow names upon the individual objects, and these names could be used in connection with the individual variables x, y, z in the logical scheme, thus applying it to the real world.[1]

To make the names useful, it would be necessary to have the power to use the same name for the same object on more than one occasion. Minimally, we must be able to use the name at a later date to refer to the object that appeared when the name was bestowed, but it would be better if we had objects that were capable of re-appearing, so that we could use the same name to refer to the object when it made its appearance for the second time. This is how we operate in ordinary language with the system of proper names, which is the model on which Russell's theory is based. I bestow the name "Fido" upon my dog and I learn to call a certain city "London," and I can use these proper names in the future to refer to the appropriate things. Russell was quite happy to concede, of course, that in our actual language objects could be introduced into

1 Bertrand Russell, *Problems of Philosophy*, chapter 5.

discourse through the use of definite descriptions like "The man in the corner," but in an ideal language the bestowing of names on objects known by acquaintance would be fundamental.

Now this system may well be unworkable, even if the objects concerned are familiar public objects like tables and chairs. But it becomes quite impossible when Russell combines it with his theory of knowledge, which puts private sense-data at the foundation. One reason for treating the objects of the primitive singular thoughts as sense-data is that since by the theory singular thoughts do not exist unless their objects exist, singular thoughts must be infallible. Because of the risk of hallucination, I cannot have a singular thought whose object is the dagger before me, since the singular thought would definitely exist, whereas the dagger may not. Thus, ordinary physical objects will be turned into logical constructions out of sense-data, and it is always possible to form a construction to which no complex will correspond. In this way, it will be possible to construct complex representations of objects which do not exist. The sense-data of which we are directly aware must exist, because otherwise there could no awareness of them.

The meaning of the names in a language I adopt could not be understood by anyone else, even in principle, when these names denote objects which are accessible only to myself. If the foundation of my language is the naming of private sense-data, it is clear that any system of symbols that rests on this foundation could not be understood by other people. If the language I use is logically private in this way, it is totally useless for the purpose of communication. At this point the game is surely up, and one is entitled to look around for another story to explain how the symbol got its meaning.

One may pause to ask whether I could even use my logically private language to communicate with myself. To be able to talk to myself is not a huge advantage if I am anxious to talk to other people, but if I am a solipsist who does not believe in the existence of other people, a theory of language that lets me talk to myself is all that I need. Because of the pernicious influence of the sense-datum theory, the threat of solipsism loomed much larger at the time Wittgenstein was writing than it does today. Wittgenstein was therefore anxious to eliminate Russell's theory as a viable account of how we can symbolize even our own internal states. Can I even use names to identify sensations that re-appear, in the way in which I thought I could use names to re-identify familiar friends, such as Roger? Can we even make sense of the notion that a *numerically identical* sensation has appeared again? I know what it means to say that the same car is back again, but when I say that the same pain is back again, I do not mean that a *numerically* identical pain has returned. The most that could be done in this language would be to use a name to refer to the past sensation on which I originally bestowed that name. If yesterday I experienced a sharp pain in the neck that I called "Roger," today I could use the word "Roger" to refer to the pain in the neck I experienced yesterday. Wittgenstein might well object to even this very minimal achievement, on the ground that in this system there would be no way to distinguish between correct and incorrect uses of this word, which is a feature available in all natural languages. How could I be sure that I was using the word to refer to the same item I called "Roger" yesterday?[2]

2 THE DESCRIPTION OF MY SENSATIONS

Using arguments along these lines, Wittgenstein can construct a conclusive demolition of the Russell theory. It would be a mistake, however, to move from this easy victory over a technical theory proposed by Russell to an attack on the common belief that I can describe, not only to myself but even to other people – sensations to which I alone have an immediate access. At the level of ordinary life, everyone naturally assumes that we can describe our sensations to other people, which is what makes any claim that we cannot do this seem so paradoxical. When the doctor asks me to describe my pain, I believe that I can tell him when I feel the pain and when I do not, and also a good deal about the special character of the pain – for example I can say whether it is dull or intense. I assume that the doctor will understand me and will assign to me sensations similar to ones that he or she has felt at some time or other. This capacity to ascribe, to others, sensations similar to those which I have felt myself is the basis of that sympathy I feel for others in distress. I feel sympathy for others because I have felt what I think they feel. I feel sympathy, not because they are being forced to writhe and shout and cry, which is not that bad, but because of the pain I imagine they are experiencing.

A language in which I describe my sensations must indeed involve terms expressing general concepts that designate specific *types* of sensations. The mistake Russell made was to attempt to devise a theory of language on the basis of an extreme nominalism in which the fundamental act was the bestowing of names upon particulars. With the collapse of this approach, the obvious move is to switch from nominalism to conceptualism, which is the traditional alternative. Once we assume general concepts as part of our original intellectual equipment, I am not only able to describe sensations of pain of which I am aware here and

2 I shall discuss the details of Wittgenstein's subtle argument later on, in the context of a much stronger theory. It would be a pity to waste it, so to speak, in order to drive one more nail into the coffin of a theory that is already on its last legs.

now, but also sensations I remember experiencing in the past and sensations I expect to experience in the future. The sensations will all have the same description because they fall under the same general concept, which is expressed in our language by the use of the word "pain." Most significantly, such concepts that derive their content from sensations directly experienced can be used to ascribe similar sensations to other people. I do not assign to another person the actual pain I may be feeling myself, but something else that falls under the same concept. Within the conceptualist model, of course, no language that I use to describe my own sensations will be *logically* private. It cannot be a language that no one else can understand, even in principle. Other people will be able to understand my description of my own sensations, if they also have sensations that fall under the same concept. The notion of a *logically* private language can be given sense, only within the context of Russell's nominalist theory.

3 SCEPTICAL DOUBTS

The story in the preceding section seems extremely plausible until the sceptic appears and introduces the worm of doubt. The successful use of a language to communicate to other people the nature of my internal sensations at a given time depends upon the assumption that these other people have experienced the same kind of sensations at some time. But how can I be absolutely sure that other people[3] really do experience sensations just like the ones I enjoy myself? When I ascribe to another person a feeling of pain, I must rely on external signs. I assign pain if the other person has suffered what would be in my own case a painful injury. I assign pain if the other person is behaving in the kind of way in which I myself behave when I am in pain. But how can I be *sure* that the other person is really enduring the kind of sensation that I myself experience in such conditions?

Ordinary caution is certainly appropriate, since there are cases where people are faking, displaying impressive pain behaviour while not feeling a thing (a reluctant warrior may put on such a display during a medical examination for military service!). But the philosophical sceptic is introducing a more general doubt, based on the impossibility of getting

---

3 Notice that in explicitly specifying "other people" I am deliberately restricting the question to members of the family of man. Individuals belonging to this biological species with hereditary ties, it seems, to the same individual may be presumed to be basically similar in most respects. It is, however, no more than a presumption that different people experience similar pains in similar circumstances.

inside the head of another person to check up on the sensations actually felt. If other people do not experience the same *kind of* sensation I feel when I say I am in pain, then they do not completely understand me, since they are not in possession of a concept with the same content as that which underlies my use of the word "pain." As I use it the word "pain" will belong to my private language, which is not, as it happens, understood by other people.

This is not to say, of course, that my private language is *logically* private, since it *could* be understood by some other person, even if this is not the case at the moment. For example, suppose that the sensation I get when I hit my thumb with a hammer is of a unique kind, because of some genetic peculiarity in my make-up; I may come to have a child with the same genetic peculiarity, who understands me completely.[4] On the other side, if other people *do* experience the same kind of sensation I feel when I hit my thumb with a hammer, then they *will* completely understand what I mean when I say that I am in pain. Thus, the mere fact that we cannot access the experiences of other people does not prove that we do not understand them when they explain the sensations they are having. So long as the sensations they feel and the sensations I feel fall under the same concept, then I do understand what they are saying.

At this point, the sceptic might move to higher ground and argue that even if I am lucky enough to understand correctly the description someone else is offering of his or her sensations, I still cannot be *sure* that I have got it right. And if I cannot be sure, I cannot *know,* for instance, that someone else is in pain. This is a familiar argument that the sceptic can deploy against most of the things we normally think we know. Inspired by Descartes, the sceptic argues that it is possible to doubt almost all my normal beliefs – not just the belief that someone who writhes and squeals in front of me is in pain, but even my conception of the things in the world around me – because of the ever-present risk of hallucination! When I am in doubt, I cannot be sure, and when I am not sure, then I do not know. The absolute certainty that the sceptic requires is indeed hard to come by, but I do not need this level of assurance to say in ordinary life that I know something. In saying that I know, I need to be sure, but only sure enough for my present purposes. What is sure enough will vary with these purposes – there are times when we have to be particularly careful and other times when we can be more cavalier. What the sceptic does is crank up the level of certainty required, in an

---

4 There are, indeed, some people who do not experience pain at all in the normal way. Such persons will have to operate with a "gutted" concept of pain, like the "gutted" concept of "yellow" assigned above to the colour-blind. See chapter 3, section 6.

unreasonable and artificial way, by exploiting our recognition that it is always possible that we are mistaken, so that in the end we may doubt everything and know nothing!

4 THE POSSIBILITY OF A PRIVATE LANGUAGE

Even if a language that I set up to describe my own sensations is not a logically private language, it is logically possible that it is a private language if no one else happens to enjoy the same kind of sensations as I do. Can I construct such a language, which no one else understands? This exploration may seem like an academic exercise to most people, who believe that we experience more or less the same sensations as others. But an alternative formulation of much the same question asks whether or not I can construct such a language without having to *presuppose* that it is understood by other people. This is precisely what Wittgenstein appears to challenge.

The argument begins by exploring the alleged predicament of a mythical individual who is attempting to set up a private language to describe the course of his or her own experience without reference to anything beyond it. The process typically begins by assigning a word or sign to some sensation and resolving to use the same word or sign whenever the same kind of sensation reappears. The rule for the use of this word is that it be applied, and applied only to a certain kind of sensation (Wittgenstein is obviously right to point out that a word can have a meaning only if we have established rules for its correct use). Now it is certainly true that the person who is developing the private language will at least make the attempt to follow the rules implicit in his choice of certain signs to designate certain kinds of experiences. Nevertheless, the question asked by Wittgenstein is this: "How can the speaker of the private language be sure that he is following his rules correctly?" I now want to use a word in my private language – "pain" – to describe a certain experience I am enjoying (in the technical sense of enjoy). But how do I know that I am using the word correctly? If I am tempted to say that it just seems to me that I am using the word consistently, Wittgenstein will pounce and proclaim that this obliterates the distinction between following the rule and seeming to follow the rule, which will undermine the very existence of the rule in question.[5]

---

5 "Whatever is going to seem to me right is right. And that only means that here we can't talk about 'right.'" Ludwig Wittgenstein, *Philosophical Investigations*, # 243.

A more elaborate answer would be to say that in past experience I remember using this same word to designate this same kind of sensation.
If the sensation is one that I have enjoyed only infrequently, and not at
all in the recent past, I may not be quite sure that I am using my word
consistently and correctly, but if the sensation is one that is both frequent and vivid, like the experience of pain, I will be quite sure that I am
using the right word.

But how do we know that our memories are veridical? Sometimes,
when we think that we remember, we later discover that we have made a
mistake. But is there a possible distinction between really remembering
and seeming to remember when there is no appeal to external corroboration? I can certainly change my mind about my past experience. Lying
comfortably in bed, I may think I remember putting the cat out for the
night, and then realize that I did not, in fact, put the cat out without having any physical manifestation of the cat to jog my memory. It may be
that it is my earlier memory of assisting the cat through the door with my
booted foot that is correct, and my later memory that I did no such thing
that is mistaken, but at least one of these memories must be non-veridi-
cal. Thus, the very possibility of *incompatible* apparent memories introduces the distinction we need between real and apparent memories.

Since the possibility of error has introduced a necessary distinction
between seeming to remember and really remembering, it follows that
my seeming to remember that I used a certain word in a certain way in
the past is no *logical* guarantee that I really did use that word in that way.
However sure I may feel that I am following the rule for the use of a word
which I originally established in my private language, I can always without self-contradiction contemplate the possibility that something has
gone wrong and that a strange inconsistency has developed in my use of
the word. Moreover, if such an inconsistency has developed, there is no
foolproof way of detecting and correcting it. We may try to correct one
memory by performing some other act of recollection, but again we have
no logical guarantee that this second act of memory is veridical. Not that
a person who checks one memory against another is in the same position
as the man who buys extra copies of the morning paper to check the
correctness of his original copy, an analogy suggested by Wittgenstein
himself.[6] There are certainly cases where it is reasonable to prefer one
memory to another, and to change one's mind about the past on this
basis. A second act of memory may not simply contradict an earlier
act: it may make intelligible the mistake that the earlier act involved. If

---

6 *Philosophical Investigations,* # 265.

I merely have a memory image of the cat roaming the house as I take my boots off, which conflicts with my earlier image of my booted foot propelling the cat through the door, then who is to say which is more likely to be correct? But if the second act of memory revises my memory of the involuntary departure of the cat, by extending it to include circumstances that I remember as taking place on the previous day, I now understand my original mistake and that it *was* a mistake!

If the speaker of a private language departs inadvertently from the rule established for the use of a word, then it will certainly be very difficult for that person to get back on track. Since there is no one else who understands my rule, there is no one else who can put me right. On the other hand, when I talk about public objects in the public language, what I have to say can be corroborated or corrected by other people. They can agree or disagree about my opinion of the facts, and they can agree or disagree about the words I have chosen to express this opinion. But although with a public world and a public language we have instruments of correction not available to people who have invented their own systems of signs to describe their own experiences, is not the difference between public and private languages in this respect more a difference in degree rather than a difference in kind? I may begin to misuse a word in our language without other people bothering to put me right and they may not even notice that I have gone astray. And if I cannot rely on other people to correct me, how can I be sure that I am using words correctly? The gist of the private language argument is that the speaker of a private language has no *criterion* of correctness, in the sense that he does not have available a reliable procedure through which he can correct, on a second pass, the mistakes that the speaker of a public language certainly makes from time to time on a first pass. But do we ever possess what amounts to a reliable *criterion* in this sense? My friend, on whom I rely to correct me, may not bother to correct me, may not notice that I need correction, and even if he does try to put me right, he may be every bit as misguided as I am myself. There is such a thing as a *folie à deux*.

To sum up, the foes of private language argue that when I use my private word for my special sensation a second time, there can be no distinction between using it correctly and using it incorrectly. They suggest that without external corroboration I cannot be *sure* that I have used my word correctly. But in many cases, I would seem to be sure enough, and in other cases, it is not clear how much external corroboration would actually help.

Even if there were never any secure basis for correcting the use of words in a private language, it surely does not follow that the use of such words could neither be correct nor incorrect. The actual relationship is the other way round. It does not make sense to talk about the possibility of correction, unless the original item is the sort of thing that could be correct or incorrect. It may be that there are cases where there is only one chance to get a thing right, and if we miss that chance, there is no way of retrieving our error. It is surely unreasonable to say that if we have only *one* chance to get a thing right, then we have *no* chance to get a thing right, and no question of correctness or incorrectness can arise. It is possible to make a mistake that there is no chance of undoing, once the mistake is made. This does not make it any less of a mistake.

5 GENERAL CONCEPTS

My general conclusion has to be that the private language argument, when it is not restricted to an attack on Russell's special theory, is unbelievably weak and inconclusive. But if I am right, why has the argument received such wide acceptance among competent philosophers? There is obviously more to the situation than meets the eye.

For a private language to be a going concern, we need a theory of language with more resources than that of Russell, where we simply bestow logically proper names upon particulars known by acquaintance. To make a private language, or indeed any language, work we must assume the possibility of constructing general concepts that can be applied to a number of distinct particulars. But what are general concepts and how can they be formed? Objective Idealism, which dominated British philosophy in the second half of the nineteenth century, assumed general concepts, called "logical ideas," as fundamental in cognition.[7] On this account, general concepts are more fundamental than language, and are required to explain the possibility of a language in which symbols are adopted through convention to express associated general concepts.

This answer to the private language argument through the introduction of concepts forged in the fire of private experience is not, however, an answer that Wittgenstein could accept. Objective Idealism, which posited logical ideas – in the sense of general ideas – as fundamental to mind was totally out of fashion in Cambridge at that time, and Russell himself had led the charge against it. There was no going back to the earlier view; another theory had to be found. The original alternative had been the Russellian theory of singular thoughts, and when this collapsed another theory had to be constructed, one which did not fall back

7 A more detailed account of Bradley's objective idealism is provided in chapter 11, section 2 and chapter 12, section 1.

into the earlier idealism. One can understand how difficult it would have been for those whose energies had been devoted to attacking and making fun of Absolute Idealism to capitulate and admit that their opponents had been essentially right all along.

Since the meanings of sentences and the meanings of the words forming sentences are clearly distinct from the physical characteristics of the signs and symbols used to express these words and sentences, how are we to explain this without returning to the *logical ideas* of idealism? In connection with the logic of *Principia Mathematica* Bertrand Russell had introduced expressions like "x is bald" which he called "propositional functions." One moved from the function to a genuine proposition by replacing the variable "x" with a reference to a real individual, such as Winston Churchill. A variety of different propositions can be constructed from the same propositional function by inserting in the function references to different individuals in place of the variable. These propositions all have something in common, which is defined by the propositional function.

Russell's theory of propositional functions can be given a Kantian spin[8] by taking seriously Kant's description of concepts as "predicates of possible judgments."[9] For Kant, judgment is the basic act of the understanding, and when we have the same predicate used in different acts of judgment, we have a common form shared by the various acts. Since the form of an act is a function, the various judgments may be said to exemplify the same propositional function. Thus, the concepts in the mind may be regarded as functions of the understanding.[10]

6 THE THEORY OF WITTGENSTEIN

Wittgenstein would not be happy with this account because it introduces concepts in the mind and functions of the understanding – a mental apparatus that Wittgenstein would prefer to do without. This is getting too close to Objective Idealism, which in fact owed a great debt to Kant's critical philosophy. Wittgenstein's strategy is to replace concepts as principles of explanation by an account of our linguistic practices. His suggestion is that the meaning of a word or sentence is the rule for the use

---

8 The Kantian spin is not mandatory, although it is a plausible alternative to settling propositional functions in a robust domain of abstract objects, with which Russell at one stage would have been quite happy. Such a domain is, of course, no more congenial to Wittgenstein than the system of Kantian mental functions.

9 *Critique of Pure Reason*, A 69 B 94.

10 "Concepts rest on functions." *Critique of Pure Reason*, A 68 B93.

of that word or sentence in the language game to which it belongs. For example, take the predicate "is bald." The meaning of that expression is the rule or criterion for its correct application to particular people, not some concept in the mind that it denotes or expresses. Wittgenstein is shifting attention away from any internal basis for the rules toward the criteria we use to determine whether different people are or are not using the same rule. The hope is that in this way we can eliminate the need to invoke any internal basis in the mind, such as concepts belonging to a special ontological category. Certainly, the words in a language cannot be reduced to the mere physical patterns constituting the symbols employed, but what there is over and above these physical patterns is the linguistic practice of a society of language users. There are rules for the correct use of words, rules not reducible to the physical properties of the symbols employed. These rules are more or less agreed upon by members of a linguistic group and they can be taught to infants entering the community of language users.

No doubt, the use of the words in our language is generally taught by our society, although we must be allowed some leeway to introduce completely new words. Unless some people at some time are allowed to coin new words, from where did we get all the words that appear in the *Oxford English Dictionary*? Allowing, however, that we have acquired the meanings of most of the words that we know from the teaching, formal or informal, of experienced language users, these words cannot be taught unless they are learned. But how is this possible? How can the young learn from the old the linguistic rules determining the meanings of words in their society? Do the young learn the rules by a kind of osmosis from a small number of examples, guided by explicit correction when they go wrong? Or is it the case that these rules cannot be learned except by an intelligent being with a capacity to construct general concepts?

Perhaps we can get an answer to this fundamental question if we turn our attention from rules for the use of words to rules for the construction of mathematical series. Wittgenstein himself is particularly partial to mathematical examples, where the participants develop series of numbers. So long as the series under construction have the same members, we may assume that the same rule is being used, but as soon as the series begin to diverge, we have to assign different rules. Two people begin "2, 4, 6, 8," but one goes on "10, 12, 14, 16," whereas the other continues "10, 14, 18, 22." It is clear that the people are using different rules once the series diverge, but have they not also been using different rules from the very beginning? Each time a term is added to the series constructed so far, the person responsible performs an act, and what makes the series a series – rather than a random succession of numbers – is that the same kind of act is performed each time. In the first case, the act is "adding two": in the second case, the rule is different and more complicated. When a series is constructed by adding two each time, each act of addition is exemplifying the same form. Since the form of an act is a function, we may say that the same function is presupposed throughout the deployment of the series. This function can indeed be represented in the language of mathematics as "$y = x+2$."

This description of the mathematical series does indeed involve a very considerable amount of ontological baggage, which many people might be reluctant to load into their theory. The series is conceived, not as a simple succession of items but as a construction, which involves an agent responsible for the construction. The gradual deployment of the series requires a succession of distinct acts of the same kind. Each act in the construction of the series is controlled by the same principle and exemplifies the same form. Thus, in addition to agents and their acts, we must also posit forms or functions.

This account of the mathematical series links directly to the question about the meaning of the general words in our language, if we make use of Russell's notion of the propositional function and the associated Kantian account of judgment mentioned at the end of section 5. The concepts that constitute the meanings of our general terms[11] are propositional functions or forms of judgment.[12] Two acts of judgment employing the same concept with respect to different individuals exemplify the same form or function (since the form of an act is a function).

In the case of the mathematical series a listing of the members, no matter how long, necessarily underdetermines the principle involved in its construction. If we are given the series "2, 4, 6, 8, 10 ...," the rule may be the simple rule of adding two each time, but it could also be the more complex rule "Add two each time until you reach ten: thereafter, add four each time," which will produce a different continuation. In the same way the actual use of some word that I observe in my linguistic group underdetermines the concept I glean from this use. The small child hears the word "doggie" used in various contexts and extracts a concept that also covers the black bear that has wandered into the camp!

---

11 I am focusing on the general terms denoted by capital letters in the predicate calculus.

12 This is, of course, to use the term "form of judgment" in a much wider sense than is our usual practice. Normally, "form of judgment" refers to a highly general, topic-neutral or logical form such as "All S are P." I am considering any expression a form of judgment so long as it contains a variable such that the expression can be turned into an actual judgment by replacing the variable with a reference to some object.

Thus, the actual practice of a group of language users does not constitute the meanings of the words employed, except insofar as we coin the
idea of an official or "dictionary" meaning. This meaning is based on the
rough agreement of the members of the group, each of whom uses
words as determined by the system of concepts that makes up his or her
idiolect. It is the conceptualization of the individual that is primary, not
the linguistic practice of the group.

Wittgenstein may say that he is following the same rule as someone
else, when there is agreement about how to go on and that he is using
the same concept as someone else, when there is agreement about what
cases to include. But he refuses to say that the agreement is to be explained by different people employing the same mental functions.
Instead, he says that this agreement is one of the extremely general facts
of nature. Perhaps we are now back to the "mystical" introduced in the
Tractatus![13] It looks like the deliberate refusal to explain something that
ought to have an explanation.

7 THE CRUCIAL QUESTION

Wittgenstein's opposition to the very idea of a private language becomes
completely intelligible once we register his account of how words get
their meaning. As we have seen, Wittgenstein believes that the meanings of our words emerge from the practices of the community of language users. Without such a community there would be no meanings
and no language. Now, the single individual, who alone can sustain a
private language, does not constitute such a community; hence, a private language is impossible!

Wittgenstein's appeal to the linguistic community as the fount of
meaning also explains why he insists, counter-intuitively, that meaning
cannot arise from a single use of a word by a single person. A word, he
believes, can have no meaning unless there is a rule for its use – there
can be no rule for its use without a regular practice, and there can be no
regular practice without more than one example. For Wittgenstein, following a rule implies *doing the same*, and what "the same" is can only be
defined by a practice in which more than one person participates. For
Wittgenstein, a rule is not a rule unless it is followed more than once,
and there cannot be merely private rules for the use of a word.

The crucial question, then, is whether or not Wittgenstein is right
about the way meaning is introduced into the universe. If he is right, the

13 *Tractatus Logico-Philosophicus.*

impossibility of a private language follows more or less as a corollary. But the general issue can be fully debated without even mentioning the possibility of describing one's own sensations.

Wittgenstein adopts the viewpoint of a spectator, observing the symbol-using practice of a linguistic group. Such a spectator will detect regular patterns of use for specific symbols, which he may identify as the "meaning" of these symbols. These patterns of use may be interconnected in various ways, as will the associated meanings. The spectator will also discover the ways in which new members are trained to follow the rules adopted by the group, as well as certain procedures used to correct members who deviate from the usual practice. Just as in Hume's theory the notion of causality is unintelligible apart from *regularities* of sequence, so for Wittgenstein the notion of meaning is unintelligible apart from *regular patterns* of use.

For Wittgenstein the description of the actual patterns of use to be found in a linguistic group is as far as we can go, just as for a Humean the end of the line is the description of the actual regularities of sequence that constitute causal connection.[14] But just as there is an instinctive desire to try to uncover the cement of the universe that explains the causal regularities, so also we naturally seek an explanation for the regularities of use that we find in a linguistic group. The suggestion I have made is that each individual speaker of the language operates with a system of concepts, which he or she learns to express through the conventional words selected in the group. Without the backing of the concept, the linguistic symbol could not have the meaning it does and could not have the use it does. Of course, there may be exceptional cases where the construction of the concept follows exposure to the word. No doubt you are now acquiring the concept of a regular triskaidekahedron, or plane figure with thirteen equal sides, because I have just used the word. But generally and fundamentally, it is the concept that comes first.

Another reason for the necessary distinction between the word and the concept it expresses is that the same concept may be expressed through the use of different words. This is the standard case when different languages are used, but even within the same language we may have different words and the same concept. There is a particularly interesting example of this when we use singular and plural sentences: "Mary is a woman," "Ann and Helen are women." Here we are using different

---

14 David Hume is not himself completely satisfied by this account and notoriously conducts an unsuccessful hunt for the origin of the idea of necessary connection that fails to emerge from the observation of the regularity of sequence. See *A Treatise of Human Nature*, book 1, part 3, section 14.

words with different rules for their use, but the concept expressed by the predicate is the same![15]

If we again take up the consideration of mathematical series, we get the same kind of result. We may observe different people producing the same strings of natural numbers, and in this way we detect a certain regularity. The rational demand is for an explanation of this regularity. One possible explanation would be that the various people are copying the strings of numbers from the same book, but if no book is to be found, we must try something else. Another possible explanation is that the various people are all following the same rule, in the sense that they are all using the same rule to generate successive members of the series. But one cannot use a rule unless one is conscious of the rule, and this means possessing the concept that constitutes the rule. One cannot produce the series "1, 2, 4, 8, 16 ..." without possessing the concept of doubling a number (or multiplying by two).[16] To explain the regularities in the construction of series and the use of words by introducing a domain of concepts in the mind of the individual cognitive subject is to pay a price, in terms of ontological inflation, which not everyone may be prepared to pay. The choice to be made is this: leave the use of language essentially unexplained, or complicate the universe by introducing concepts and robust cognitive subjects with the power to conceptualize their universe!

A serious problem facing the supporters of the private language argument is the presence in our language of a large vocabulary of terms purporting to refer to what is going on in our inner life. This was handled by the strategy of *logical behaviourism*, which was designed to alter the "logical geography" of our system of mental concepts. The most brilliant example of such a strategy is *The Concept of Mind* by Gilbert Ryle. I have argued against Ryle's position in a recent book and I shall not repeat my arguments here.[17] Suffice to say that if Wittgenstein's position is rejected, there is no need for a theory that explains the rules for the use of mental concepts in terms of situation and behaviour. We are entitled to construct propositions that assign mental states, using concepts with a

15 "Singular and plural forms of nouns express no difference of concept; the difference is essentially semantical, not conceptual." Henry Laycock, "The Matter of Objects," section 5.

16 This is not completely accurate, since it may be possible to construct this very series through the use of a different function. Another way is to construct the next term by adding together all the antecedent terms and adding one. It is possible that different functions may determine the same series, in the same way that different concepts may refer to the same object, e.g. "the morning star" and "the evening star." I owe this point to Torin Doppelt.

17 *Why Consciousness is Reality*, 25–7.

stuffing acquired in immediate experience. Although my criteria for ascribing pain to other people may depend on my perception of their behaviour and situation, the core of what I believe is that they are experiencing an unpleasant inner state of a kind with which I am only too familiar in my own case.[18]

8 PRIVATE LANGUAGE AGAIN

If we adopt the essentially Kantian position that the rule for the use of a word depends on a concept that is a form or function of the understanding, then there is no reason why there cannot be perfectly meaningful words used only once. For Kant, it is possible to make only once a judgment that employs a certain concept, even if the *possibility* of using the same concept again is entailed by its generality. Moreover, there is no reason why the rule for the use of a word and the associated concept cannot cover entities that are not accessible to anyone else. This vindicates the intuitive conviction, explored in section 4, that a private language in which I attach my own symbols to the concepts I apply to my own sensations is perfectly feasible. We are now explicitly aware, however, of the ontological cost involved in maintaining this intuition, and those who are not willing to pay the price will have to discard the intuition.

When we are dealing, not with concepts in the mind, but with words in the natural language, it is reasonable to suggest that we normally talk about things in the public world that we share with other speakers of the language, and not about our own private sensations. One might even concede that we could not learn to describe our inner experiences to other people until we had learned to describe public objects in the language we share with our society.[19] For example, I experience a certain unpleasant odour, but cannot describe it to other people until I identify it as the smell of a skunk. Without the vocabulary to communicate with other people about the kind of creature responsible for the smell, I cannot tell other people exactly what I am experiencing. Of course, I can form a concept of this kind of smell without having a concept of a skunk, and I can even invent a word in a private language to express this concept. But apart from an inspired guess other people will not understand

18 This eminently sensible position depends, of course, on the argument from analogy, which I defend against criticism in the next chapter.

19 This concession, as we have seen above (18–19), is perfectly compatible with the weakened version of the traditional theory of perception, since this version does not insist that the pattern of inference at the heart of the traditional theory is our *original* source of knowledge of the external world.

what I refer to when I use my special word (as a matter of fact, other people do not have to be *that* inspired to guess the meaning of the word in my private language if they are having a vivid experience of the same kind of distinctive smell – as people are wont to do when a skunk has been in operation).[20]

The positing of concepts that have their foundation in personal experience rather than in the language employed in one's society respects the element of truth in what Russell and his friends were getting at in their sense-datum theory. Certainly, it will not do to trace the origin of language to the bestowing of names on sensations. Nevertheless, there is something to be said for the conviction of the traditional empiricists that it is our sensations or impressions that provide the stuffing for the empirical concepts we share with our fellows and express in the language through which we describe the world. This stuffing is essential, although it is not essential that different people use the same stuffing for the concept associated with the same word.[21]

9 CONCLUSION

I have found it necessary to spend a good deal of time on the private language argument because of its importance in philosophy today. If I have been successful in disarming this argument, I have removed one serious obstacle to operating the pattern of inference at the heart of the traditional theory of perception. We can identify and describe the sensations produced in us by external objects and therefore have available the premises necessary to infer the external objects responsible. For example, I can recognize two extended regions immediately experienced in the visual field as the same colour, when they are. If there are two patches of yellow, I can recognize them as both yellow. Even if I experience only a single yellow patch, I can imagine another patch exactly the same colour appearing in the future.

To vindicate the premises employed in the traditional pattern is, however, no more than half the battle. The other problem is to justify the inferences that take us beyond the premises to a knowledge of the external world. Such inferences can be justified only if we *assume* a system of things in space and time endowed with causal powers, including the

---

20 At a later time, I may, of course, integrate this fragment of private language in the public discourse, by finding out what word the public seems to use for this kind of olfactory sensation; but it is also possible that I never learn to carry out this translation from my private language to the language of the group.

21 See the discussion of *inverted qualia* in chapter 3, section 5.

power to produce sensations in subjects of experience. The central thesis of the first part of this work has two components. First, the system of causally organized objects in space and time presupposed by the traditional pattern of inference cannot be established by this pattern, since this would be circular. Second, this presupposition is in fact true and is recognized as true by all right-thinking people. The operation of the traditional pattern of inference is therefore justified.

If the original belief in a system of external objects required to operate the traditional pattern cannot be reached by an inference from sensations, it must be acquired in some other way. What is this other way? As I have already explained, the defence of the pattern of inference involved in the traditional theory of perception does not require me to find this other way. It is sufficient for me to believe, with everyone else, that there must be another way! The problem of the other way emerging from my limited defence of the traditional theory is no different from the problem of perception facing those who ignore the traditional theory completely. Nevertheless, in the second part of this work, I shall launch an attack upon this formidable problem. This can be regarded as a fresh start by those who wish to forget everything I have said in Part One.

6

Other Minds

Before we attack the central problem of Part Two, there is one more topic with which we must deal. This topic is the existence of other minds. I have been assuming without question that I share this world with other conscious beings like myself. Indeed, I would not even be writing this book unless I thought that there were other intelligent beings who might read and understand it. I have explained the problem of Part Two as the problem of how we originally acquire the empirical knowledge of an external world which is presupposed by the operation of the pattern of inference in the traditional theory of perception. But what right do I have to talk about "we"? Strictly, should I not be talking just about myself?

The account I have been giving depends upon a robust conception of the experiences and other internal states of the perceiving subject. In order to protect this conception in the preceding chapter, I was forced to take on the arguments of Wittgenstein and his associates, which threaten such a conception of one's own internal states. It is not enough, however, for me to explain how I can ascribe to myself internal states of belief and desire, feeling and sensation. It is also necessary for me to explain how I can generalize from my own case to other persons who also enjoy beliefs and desires and so on. How is it possible for me to ascribe the kind of conscious experience that I enjoy to certain favoured beings important in my environment? I see around me, and interact with other human beings; I assume without question that these other human beings also have conscious experiences. But I have no direct access to the experiences of other people. The inner life of other people is more deeply hidden than even their physical bodies, which I do seem to be able to represent through their effect on my senses. How can I be sure that there really is a mind or consciousness lying behind that friendly face? Traditionally, these worries have been laid to rest by an appeal to the argument from analogy.

2 THE ARGUMENT FROM ANALOGY

I notice that my body with its activities is similar to other human bodies with their activities. Since I know from the inside that there is a conscious experience associated with my own body, I infer that there are similar experiences associated with other bodies like my own. There is always the logical possibility that my friend is a philosophical zombie, totally devoid of any form of consciousness, but able to simulate the exact behaviour of a real human being. This mere logical possibility is not, however, a real worry – a more serious concern is to determine if consciousness has departed when someone appears to be in a deep coma, since there may be a real possibility that consciousness is still there even though systems of communication with the external world have all broken down.

In recent philosophy, the argument from analogy has been understood as a way of encouraging me to ascribe consciousness to other beings like myself. Historically, however, the ideas behind it were more necessary to cut back on the rampant assignment of cognition, agency, and consciousness all over the place. Primitive man tended to assume, for instance, that the sun was a conscious being with emotions and cognitions and purposes, interacting with the world below. The Sun was turned into the Sungod! Scientific knowledge and the argument from analogy put a stop to that.

There is, indeed, a question about how far we may go in assigning some kind of consciousness to other creatures resembling ourselves *to some degree* in form and behaviour. What about cats and dogs? Descartes was adamant in refusing conscious experience to all other animals, but he had special reasons for adopting this counterintuitive position.[1] Descartes was never required to face up to the question of the Neanderthals and missing links connecting us to monkeys, discovered through anthropological research since his day. His answer, no doubt, would depend on whether he conceived of such creatures as stupid human beings,[2] in which case a rational soul would be attached, or as very clever apes, in which case they would be mere machines.

1 Descartes' theory assigned consciousness to an immaterial and immortal soul, and he did not want to provide dogs with a place in heaven.

2 Neanderthals, it now appears, were not that stupid, and their disappearance was not necessarily due to stupidity.

How far we may go down the Great Chain of Being and still find associated with the creatures something that we can reasonably call consciousness is a question that appears to have no clear answer – we are reduced to an informed guess, perhaps a mere guess.[3] But even when we argue by analogy to determine the inner life of other creatures in human form, our inferences are often quite shaky. I will assume that other people watching and hearing a child in distress will share my feelings of concern, but I can easily be wrong. Even when the other people make suitable noises, it is more than a logical possibility that these noises are simulated. I also assume that other people, when they look at the green grass or the blue sky above, enjoy the same colour experiences as I do. But as we have seen, this is by no means guaranteed.[4]

One objection to the argument from analogy is that it rests on a very narrow base (essentially, the single case of my own conscious experience). The base can, however, be expanded through introducing the dimension of time. For example, I felt a pain in my tooth yesterday, I do not feel it today, but I fear I may feel it again tomorrow. There is a distinction among the self of tomorrow, the present self, and the self of yesterday (there has to be, to avoid contradiction!). We have a variety of *logical* subjects to which the concept of consciousness can be ascribed without having to step outside to bring in other minds. I assume that the self of tomorrow will have much the same sort of experiences as the self of today. When tomorrow comes, there are no surprises, at least not about this.

Certainly, it is hard to be as secure as one would be with a more broadly based argument. How can I be sure, for example, that other people who seem to experience pain are feeling the same sort of thing as I feel myself? I do seem to be sure enough for practical purposes, since my conviction that other people suffer the same pains and experience the same joys as I do myself is at the heart of my moral concern for their welfare. Nevertheless, the worries of the philosophical sceptic are not without their impact.

3 THE STRAWSON OBJECTION

A more fundamental objection, however, has been developed in recent years to the very conceptual framework in which the argument from analogy must be expressed. A classical and influential version is given by P.F. Strawson and is to be found in his book *Individuals*, chapter 3,

3 There is further discussion of this point in chapter 12, section 4: "Primitive Cognition."

4 See chapter 3, section 5.

section 4.[5] The chapter is entitled "Persons," and part of section 4 deals with what Strawson calls the Cartesian view.[6]

The expression "the Cartesian view" contains an important ambiguity. One may be thinking of the point of departure in the "cogito" (I think), or one may be thinking of Descartes' metaphysical conclusion – the strict dualism of mental and material substances. The "cogito" expresses the thought that there is an original and indubitable consciousness of self as subject of experience. Descartes goes on to draw the conclusion that this conscious subject is a thinking substance necessarily distinct from the material substances occupying space, but the argument to this conclusion is far from compelling. It is possible to accept the Cartesian "cogito" while rejecting Cartesian dualism. This would certainly be the case for the panpsychism of G.W. Leibniz or Alfred North Whitehead. Even a materialist might accept an original consciousness of self as primitive, while maintaining that in the last analysis this self-conscious being was nothing but a certain configuration of material particles.

Strawson certainly joins in the general rejection of the Cartesian dualism of mind and matter, but he also launches a more controversial attack on the fundamental Cartesian principle, the "I think." This attack, if successful, would knock out the very foundation of the entire Cartesian system, but it would also destroy the traditional argument from analogy, which seems to be the most natural way to establish the existence of other minds. Strawson is attacking the contention that there is an original act of self-consciousness, in virtue of which the subject can ascribe to himself the variety of experiences he enjoys. If he is right, I cannot begin by affirming my own existence as subject of experience and *then* move to locate other subjects of experience connected with appropriate bodies, as the argument from analogy would require.

But how can Strawson reject what the Cartesian malignant demon with all his powers could not make false? "I think" is the one principle capable of withstanding the wiles of the very powerful deceiver. It is logically incoherent for me to doubt that I think and exist, because to doubt is to think and exist. Strawson does not deny this: he allows that I can form a concept of myself as a pure individual consciousness, as the mere subject of my experiences. Moreover, once the concept is formed, the existence of the self cannot be coherently denied.

---

5 Among those who take seriously Strawson's argument is Richard Rorty. Cf. *Philosophy and the Mirror of Nature*, 20.

6 The material in this section draws heavily on my article "Strawson and the Argument for Other Minds," 149–57.

Strawson's ingenious argument is that although this concept of the self is perfectly legitimate, it is not logically primitive. It is parasitic on the more fundamental concept of a *person*, where a person is a basic particular to which we can properly ascribe both experiences and physical predicates like height and weight. Thus, the concept of a mere subject of experience or ego is really the concept of a disembodied person. It is a mistake to suppose that the concept of the person – the bearer of both mental and physical properties – is formed by putting together the concept of an individual consciousness and the concept of its associated body.

Thus, although I cannot doubt the *truth* of the principle that I think, I can doubt that it is a primitive proposition presupposing nothing beyond itself. And if what is presupposed is precisely what the argument from analogy is supposed to reach as a conclusion, this will be just as fatal to the argument as a more radical thesis that denies the very significance of the cogito. It will be no help to allow a legitimate concept of the Cartesian ego, if that concept cannot be available at the time it is required to infer the existence of other people. The crucial question is whether Strawson can show that the ascription of states of consciousness to myself, which is the starting point for the argument from analogy, has presuppositions that sabotage its use in this argument.

4 STRAWSON'S CENTRAL ARGUMENT

Strawson summarizes his central argument as follows: "One can ascribe states of consciousness to oneself only if one can ascribe them to others. One can ascribe them to others only if one can identify other subjects of experience. And one cannot identify others if one can identify them *only* as subjects of experience, possessors of states of consciousness" (100). The first sentence expresses a crucial assumption that Strawson calls "a very central thought" when he introduces a variant at an earlier point: "it is a necessary condition of one's ascribing states of consciousness, experiences, to oneself, in the way one does, that one should also ascribe them, or be prepared to ascribe them, to others who are not oneself" (99).

According to the argument from analogy, the act of ascribing states of consciousness to oneself is an act that must take place *before* one goes on to ascribe similar states to other beings in the environment. Strawson is contending that these acts cannot take place in the order required. If he could affirm categorically that the *actual* ascription of consciousness to others is a necessary condition of its ascription to oneself, his case would be established. Strawson backs away from this stronger claim by allowing that it is enough if one is "prepared" to ascribe states of consciousness to others. But this weaker thesis no longer appears strong enough to destroy the argument from analogy. Supporters of that argument may *begin* by ascribing states of consciousness to themselves, but they are certainly *prepared* to ascribe such states to others. They *demonstrate* their willingness to do so when they carry out their inference to other centres of consciousness.

It is not as simple as this, however. Certainly, the person who uses the argument from analogy is prepared to ascribe states of consciousness to others, in the sense of possessing the requisite concept of consciousness, which in view of its generality one cannot appropriate for one's own case alone. But can such a person be said to be *fully* prepared to ascribe states of consciousness to others, unless he or she is also able to identify other subjects to whom the states can be ascribed? The idea is that there are *two* necessary conditions of the ascription of states of consciousness to others. I call one the *conceptual* condition: one can ascribe states of consciousness to others only if one possesses the general concept of conscious state. I call the other the *referential* condition: one can ascribe states of consciousness to others only if one has a way of identifying the individuals to whom the concept may be applied. One is fully prepared to ascribe states of consciousness to others only when both conditions are satisfied. The same distinction can be drawn in the case of every special kind of conscious or psychical state. For example, I can ascribe beliefs to others only if I possess a general concept of belief (conceptual condition) and a way of identifying individuals to whom the concept may be applied (referential condition).

The clear distinction between the two necessary conditions reveals the ambiguity on which Strawson's argument depends. The first two premises are as follows:[7] "*One can ascribe states of consciousness to oneself, only if one can ascribe them to others. One can ascribe them to others only if one can identify other centres of experience.*" The second premise clearly specifies the referential condition, whereas the condition involved in the first premise is the conceptual condition. To make the nature of the paralogism more evident, I shall reconstruct the argument to incorporate the justification that Strawson offers for the first premise: "*One can ascribe conscious states to oneself, only if one possesses a general concept of consciousness. One possesses a general concept of consciousness, only if one is prepared to ascribe conscious states to others. One is prepared to ascribe conscious states to others, only*

---

7 I am ignoring for the time being the third proposition constituting Strawson's central argument: "one cannot identify others, if one can identify them, *only* as subjects of experience." My strategy is to invalidate Strawson's critique of the argument from analogy by finding a flaw in its earlier stages.

if one has a way of identifying other centres of consciousness." The argument appears plausible, but it collapses once the distinction between two levels of preparation is clearly drawn. The level of preparation indicated in the second premise is not the same as the level of preparation indicated in the third. In the second premise, one is prepared only to the extent that one has the general concept available, so that one has satisfied the conceptual condition. In the third premise, one is prepared to the extent that one has available, specifiable individuals to whom the general concept may be applied, satisfying the referential condition.

The only way to save the argument would be to show that there is a logical connection between the two conditions, such that the conceptual condition is satisfied only if the referential condition is also satisfied. In an important note, Strawson suggests that there is such a logical connection and that what we have here is at bottom a purely logical point: "the idea of a predicate is correlative with that of a *range* of distinguishable individuals of which the predicate can be significantly, though not necessarily truly, affirmed" (99).

By and large, the logical point is well taken. A general concept is essentially the predicate of a possible judgment, and the idea of a possible judgment involving a certain predicate introduces the concept of possible subjects of such a judgment.[8] Cases can even be produced where the predicate concept does determine an appropriate domain or limited "*range* of distinguishable individuals of which the predicate can be significantly, though not necessarily truly, affirmed." This would seem to be true in the case of the concept of prime number. For the concept of prime number, the appropriate range is the set of natural numbers, some of which are prime and some of which are not. We do have criteria that allow us to distinguish among the various natural numbers belonging to this range.

In the same way, the concept of conscious person introduces a domain of persons, some of whom are conscious and some of whom are not (because they have been knocked unconscious, or are in a coma, or in a deep sleep). Persons belonging to this range will be distinguished, through their physical characteristics, as occupying different portions of physical space. The Cartesian principle is not, however: "I think, therefore, I am a conscious *person*." Indeed such a principle, with "person" used in the way Strawson understands it, would be a complete betrayal of the entire Cartesian approach!

---

8 I can appeal here to the authority of Immanuel Kant in the *Critique of Pure Reason*: "But concepts, as predicates of possible judgments, relate to some representation of a not *yet* determined object" (A 69 B94).

To suppose that the premise of the argument for analogy is that I am a conscious person would be to beg the argument in favour of the Strawson position. We require a more non-committal premise: "I am a conscious *being.*" Without a more specific "backing" concept such as the concept of "person," the individuals conceived as possible subjects of consciousness are represented in an indeterminate way, so that their representation as distinct individuals does not involve the possession of some actual method for identifying and distinguishing them.[9] We can introduce a specific *range* of distinguishable individuals only when the specification of the range is built into a *specific* concept that has been associated with the concept of consciousness.

The position, as I see it, is this. The ascription of states of consciousness to others does indeed require the satisfaction of both the conceptual and the referential conditions. We need both the general concept and a *range* of possible candidates for consciousness. To ascribe consciousness to myself, however, I need the general concept but *not* the range. I do indeed need a direct line to the individual I call "myself." Without the introduction of the individual, there is no judgment. But I do not require a way of introducing *other* individuals. This is to be supplied at a later stage in the argument from analogy, after the first stage – the ascription of consciousness to myself – is already in place.

5 IDENTIFYING OTHER MINDS

Although the first step in the argument from analogy – the ascription of the concept of consciousness to myself – does not imply possession of some method for identifying and distinguishing *other* individuals to which the concept might be applied, to carry the argument to its conclusion does require such a method. Through immediate self-consciousness, I am able to apply the concept of consciousness and other mental predicates to a single unique subject, that is, myself.[10] The method I use to introduce the subject of the judgment furnishes a single, specific being. There is no need to build into this method a way of distinguishing this

9 Strawson's own concept of the individual is indeed this indeterminate idea: "anything whatever can appear as logical subject, as individual," 227.

10 Kant provides a formidable account of how this is possible in the *Critique of Pure Reason* (B 131–6). The cognitive subject is introduced through an act of pure apperception, expressed through the formula "I am" or "I think" (cogito). This act affirms *that* I am: to determine *what* I am a manifold must be given in inner sense. This manifold must be combined through the unity of apperception, if I am to represent my conscious states as *mine* and the identity of the consciousness associated with these states. This account, right or wrong, certainly operates without introducing other centres of consciousness.

being from other beings enjoying conscious states, since these other beings are, so to speak, "over the horizon." At a later point, we may, indeed,
develop methods to determine what lies beyond the horizon, but such
methods are not presupposed by, nor involved in, the original determination of the subject of immediate experience.

The tension is that the generality of the concept of consciousness entails the possibility of applying this concept to other centres of consciousness, whereas I have no way of accessing any such entities in the way in
which I can access myself and my own states. In the initial phase required
by the argument from analogy conscious states are restricted to myself
alone, since all the experiences with which I am familiar are *my* experiences. This means that other possible subjects of consciousness must be
represented in a totally indeterminate fashion. It is only when the argument from analogy has got under way at a later stage in my intellectual
development that I am able to exploit this indeterminate possibility and
find a way to discriminate other centres of consciousness. I can do this
when I notice an analogy between the body I find associated with my
consciousness and certain other physical bodies around me. I associate a
mind distinct from myself with each of these other bodies.

The nature of this association between the mind and the body is, as
they say, "not at present well understood." Colin McGinn has argued,
indeed, that we cannot understand the connection between the mind
and the body, because we just do not possess the requisite concepts.[11]
This may be unduly defeatist: I make a determined attempt myself to
deal with the problem in my recent book *Why Consciousness Is Reality*.
Nevertheless, we can accept the existence of the association, even if we
are not able to explain it. Descartes himself firmly believed in an inti-
mate connection between the mind and the body – in spite of adopting
a strict metaphysical dualism, which seemed to rule it out.

6 *Persons*

We may now retrieve the third premise of the original Strawson argument. "And one cannot identify others [other subjects of experience]
if one can identify them *only* as subjects of experience, possessors of
states of consciousness." This pronouncement does indeed contain an
element of truth. To introduce other centres of consciousness in addition to myself, I must represent them as existing elsewhere in other
regions distinct from that in which I find myself. The bare posit of

11 See *The Problem of Consciousness*.

other subjects of experience similar to but numerically distinct from my conscious self will not do. Strawson wants to argue that to ascribe consciousness to others is to ascribe consciousness to other *persons*, where a person is an individual to whom both mental and physical predicates can be ascribed. This does not, however, follow. The argument from analogy identifies other minds *through* the associated physical bodies, but refuses to identify the mind with the body through which it is identified. It may well be that the required association with physical bodies requires us to assign some sort of spatial character to minds as belonging to an order of co-existence,[12] but this does not mean that the mind must occupy space in the same way we conceive physical bodies. Nor does the use of human bodies to locate other minds require us to reassign the properties of the mind to individuals who also possess the properties of bodies.

I have conceded that it is not easy to understand the connection between the mind and the body, but it seems equally difficult to understand how the same individual can combine mental and physical properties that are so radically different. The theory of persons may be thought to have the advantage of precluding any fantasy of separating the mind from the body, but we can rule out the possibility of separating the mind from its home in the body without going to such extremes.

12 I argue for this very point in *Why Consciousness Is Reality*, chapter 6. See note 11.

PART TWO

7

The Origin of Empirical Belief

1 INTRODUCTION

It now appears that in Part One we have re-instated the traditional causal representative theory of perception apart from one thing – albeit one big thing. We can now understand its attraction and the ways in which the theory of the learned is superior to the theory of the vulgar, to use the language of Hume. We can acknowledge sensations, or impressions, or experiences produced in us by external causes, which they represent but do not necessarily resemble. What we do not have is an explanation of how empirical beliefs about the external world are originally acquired, since these beliefs must be already in place before we can operate the traditional system.

This is no doubt a great disappointment for those who may have hoped that the traditional theory would provide the solution to the central problem of perception. But those who are prepared to settle for the reduced version of the theory that I have been expounding are in fact no worse off than those who would reject the theory entirely. Both groups are equally faced with the problem of explaining the original emergence of sound beliefs about the world around us, and any solution found may be equally available to both groups.

At the beginning of the book I described perception as the process by which we somehow or other acquire beliefs about the external world on the basis of an input from that external world fed in through the senses. We use these beliefs to guide our actions, to achieve our objectives, and to avoid the dangers which threaten us. According to this account, perception begins with objects affecting our senses and generating a process through which, somehow or other, sensory input is worked up to arrive at a knowledge of the external objects that were originally responsible for that input. This seems fair enough as far as it goes, but the problem of perception appears when we attempt to explain exactly how the input of sense is worked up into a knowledge of the external world. This turns out to be a problem of peculiar difficulty, because the discourse in which the initial phases of the process are described is radically different from the discourse in which we report the outcome of the process. The discourse in which the initial phases are set out is the discourse of normal science, using concepts such as light waves, eyes, retinas, nerve impulses, and states of the brain. The discourse that we use for the final phase is very different, since it introduces intentional states that involve concepts like acts of judgment, states of belief, reference to objects, truth or falsity, and so on. There is a gap, which cannot be papered over with vague phrases like "somehow or other."

Since the problem exists at the interface between distinct conceptual schemes, it is therefore a classic example of what J.J. Russell called "dialectical" problems in his book *Analysis and Dialectic.* Dialectical problems emerge at the interface between distinct conceptual systems. For different purposes we operate with different conceptual schemes that are not well integrated; the central task of philosophy is not the mere analysis of concepts, but the elucidation of the connections among our various conceptual systems. This is not easy, because we cannot rely exclusively on the concepts developed within any special scheme.

We may certainly think of the relation between our beliefs and the physiological processes that underlie them as some kind of causal relation, because these beliefs tend to vary with changes in a basis described in physiological terms. The problem is to explain how such causal relations are possible, where the antecedents are physical processes and the consequents are judgments and beliefs. We are much more comfortable with causal relations connecting things of the same type, such as the causal connections involved in mechanical processes.

2 BOTTOM UP

We may try to explore the causal connection between the physiology and the beliefs beginning at either end. We can approach the problem of perception from the bottom up or from the top down. The bottom up approach begins with the impact of external causes on the sensory system and traces the route taken by nerve impulses coming, say, from the eyes or the ears to reach the brain. It identifies the regions of the brain affected by the input from various senses and in some cases the specific changes in the brain produced by specific stimuli. This investigation is carried out entirely within the province of neurophysiology. But no matter how far we push these researches, we never arrive at anything that might be regarded as knowledge of the external world. If we persist in tracking the train of impulses, the signal going in starts to come out again in order to control the muscles we use in our response. Consciousness and cognition are completely bypassed.

The problem may become clearer if we choose a simple, concrete example. Suppose I am sitting in a radio studio and as soon as the red light comes on I must begin my recitation of "The Rime of the Ancient Mariner" by Samuel Taylor Coleridge. The onset of the red light is certainly distinct from and precedes my beginning to speak, but can we so easily distinguish the physiological processes leading up to the experience of the red flash from the processes controlling the operation of the vocal chords? When I become aware of the red light, I recognize it as the trigger stipulated by the producer, and decide to begin to speak. I can use this story to distinguish the physiological processes that lead up to my experience of red from the processes through which my decision to speak is enacted.

In many respects this is a useful and workable distinction. There are physiological processes that are generated by the stimulation of the outer body and bring the information to the brain. We may call this the "afferent" system. By contrast, the "efferent" system contains those processes in the nervous system that control the operation of the relevant muscles. Impulses emerge from the brain and pass along the motor nerves to modify the muscles controlling parts of the body. Lying between the afferent processes feeding into the brain and the efferent processes emerging from it, there is a confusing jungle of processes that operate as a kind of central processing unit. The boundaries demarcating the three segments within the physiological process are by no means rigid and might be drawn in different places. Some items originally assigned to the central processing unit might be transferred to either the afferent or the efferent divisions, if there is reason to do so.

This may suggest the idea of a complete partition of the central division between the afferent and the efferent. This would involve finding what Daniel Dennett calls a "continental divide" between the afferent and the efferent, a watershed where the inbound processes turn around and begin to come the other way.[1] This is a tall order. The extreme complexity of the central processes is so far from being understood in detail that there is at present no practical possibility of disentangling what precedes a given experience from what belongs to the response that is guided by the experience. The trains of nerve impulses belonging to the

1 *Consciousness Explained*, 108.

afferent and efferent systems can be mapped with reasonable certainty. But the centre is, as I have said, a confusing jungle where often the best we can do is merely determine which regions of the brain are most strongly activated at any given time, in connection with some specific input or output.[2]

Even if the relevant brain activity were delineated in complete detail, we would still have to pinpoint the specific process in the brain most closely associated with the experience of the red flash. And even if a way could be found to do this, we would be no closer to understanding how the experience is precipitated by the physiological process. The gap between what we report in our experience and what we discover through neurophysiology remains as wide as ever. From the point of view of physiology, the traditional problem of perception has been replaced by an attempt to explain in detail how what is fed into the central processing unit or brain[3] system is digested so as to produce the specific activity taking place in the efferent system.

In my original formulation of the problem of perception, I stated that the question is to explain how we reach beliefs about the external world on the basis of the sensory input fed in through the senses. The only way to close the gap from the bottom up would be to reduce empirical beliefs to dispositions to behave in specific ways in specific circumstances, where the categorical basis is thought to be a cluster of physiological states. This resembles Locke's redescription of the colour properties of physical objects as powers or dispositions to produce certain sensations in the minds of perceiving subjects. This way of reducing beliefs to mere functional states cannot, however, be permitted. If I believe that there is a blue ball in front of my eyes, my belief may lead me to behave in certain ways, but it also involves a certain concept with a stuffing derived from my experience of blue. If I side with the vulgar, I shall conceive the ball as having the very colour I experience; if I side with the learned, I shall assign to the ball the power to produce in normal circumstances the kind of sensation I am now getting. In both cases, the actual colour experienced is essentially involved in the belief.

This means that if we are to be able to explain the acquisition of beliefs through perception, we must be able to explain the emergence of

2 This is done by measuring increased blood flow in specific areas of the brain.

3 It is worth noting that the grey matter inside the skull is uniformly called "the brain" by philosophers and scientists, whereas in ordinary language it is quite common to talk about "the brains." Cf. "Use your brains!" This may have some significance. To identify the mind with the brains seems strange, because the very language deprives the grey matter of the unity which it needs for this identification!

conscious experiences on the basis of the physiological processes that underlie them. This is the truly formidable problem because the gap is so huge. Conscious experience is known from the inside and expressed through first-person reports, while physiological processes are known from the outside and described from an objective third-person point of view. It is hard to conceive how the gap might be closed.

To understand the impossibility of a reductive explanation of experience in terms of physiology, it is worth considering an illuminating account provided by David Chalmers. The first premise in his argument is: "Third-person data are data about the objective structure and dynamics of physical systems."[4] The second premise states that explanations in terms of such processes explain only further processes of this sort. Since conscious experiences are not processes of this sort, they cannot be explained in terms of the third-person data. This account is extremely useful, because it puts clothes on the bare intuition that there is a gap that cannot be closed.

Chalmers does not, however, wish to sweep aside all the important research done by those who may have wanted to reduce consciousness to physiology. Instead, he reinterprets the investigations of cognitive scientists working in this area as a search for what he calls the neural correlate of consciousness. According to Chalmers a "science of consciousness will not reduce first-person data to third-person data, but it will articulate the systematic connections between them. Where there is systematic covariation between two classes of data, we can expect systematic principles to underlie and explain the covariation" (40). Chalmers calls these *bridging* principles.

Certainly, the brain as a whole is a neural system that somehow supports consciousness – but we would like to get more detailed connections. Chalmers explains a neural correlate of consciousness as "a minimal neural system that is directly associated with states of consciousness" (44). The idea is to isolate limited neural systems correlated with specific types of consciousness, such as visual consciousness, and, if possible, to link variations in the neural correlates to variations in the conscious experience. This seems to be the best we can do, beginning from the bottom up.

4 *The Character of Consciousness,* 39.

3 TOP DOWN

The top-down approach begins at the other end. It begins with the achieved knowledge of the empirical world and works back to the conditions of its possibility. This is, of course, to beg the question against the extreme sceptic who would put in doubt our commonsense beliefs about the world in which we live; but it is surely not unreasonable to begin with the assumption that our normal beliefs about the external world are, by and large, correct. We can push the sceptical doubts to the back of the mind, where they can be safely quarantined until and unless there is a better reason to take them seriously than the bare fact that they can be entertained.

One version of the top-down method is to look for the source and justification of particular empirical beliefs by finding other beliefs from which they can be inferred. Our system of beliefs about the external world is structured in such a way that there are some beliefs that depend upon others, from which they have been inferred. I can explain and justify my belief that there is a skunk in the neighbourhood by showing that it is inferred from my recognition of the characteristic smell skunks are accustomed to make. I can give the basis for my belief that there is a fierce dog inside the house by pointing out that I hear the sound of barking coming from that direction. I have evidence for a belief that I have seriously damaged my car, if I hear an expensive noise when backing up.

This may appear like the early stages of the argument through which the traditional theory of perception was introduced, but there is a very significant difference. In the traditional theory, the smells and sounds upon which are founded our beliefs about the skunk and the dog are private effects in the perceiver, forged deep within the soul through an extensive processing of the sensory input by the nervous system and the brain. These are the items I have called sensations, and I have argued that an inference from these sensations to their external causes is perfectly legitimate. The snag is that such inferences cannot be carried out until our standard beliefs in a system of external objects organized through causal law have been already established.

The inferences I have introduced in the top-down approach are not, however, inferences from sensations to external objects, but inferences from a smell to what is making the smell and from a noise to what is making the noise. The smell made by the skunk is not regarded as an olfactory sensation that can be perceived only by a single subject – this smell is unfortunately available to the general public. The noise made by the dog is not something that exists only in my mind – it has the capacity to annoy many people.[5]

One can try to offer a systematic account of this procedure by using a distinction between what is inferred and what is perceived. It is clear that we have many empirical beliefs about what exists beyond the present range of the senses. I may have perceived my house as I left this morning, I may now remember that it *was* there, but how do I know that it is still there and will still be there when I get home tonight? These beliefs must depend on some kind of inference, even if it is a bit much to glorify the mental move with the title of "inference." It would be more natural to say that I assume or take for granted that my house will still be there when I get back tonight.

There is a well-established vocabulary, using words like "see," "hear," "taste," and "smell," in which we attribute what we may call "acts of perception" to human beings.[6] It would be simple if we could draw our distinction between perceiving and inferring by using the distinction between what we *say* we perceive and what we believe without the benefit of a present perception, where we cannot say we perceive. Unfortunately, even the examples I have used so far will rule this out. I have argued that the smell is perceived and the skunk is inferred, the barking noise is perceived and the dog is inferred. Nevertheless, in ordinary language it is perfectly natural to say things like: "I smell a skunk" or "I hear a dog." What then do I really smell? Is it the skunk or the smell produced by its spray? What do I really hear? Is it the dog or the sound produced by its barking?

The goal of the top-down approach, as I conceive it, is to uncover the fundamental perceptions that serve as the foundations for the inferences through which we construct our knowledge of the world around us. We cannot allow what we say in ordinary language to control our results. In the last analysis, we smell smells, not skunks. We hear noises, not dogs. We can, indeed, placate the ordinary user of the language by allowing a sense in which it may be true to say that I smell a skunk and hear a dog. These sentences are acceptable if we construe them as elliptical. They become: "I smell (a smell made by) a skunk" and "I hear (a sound made by) a dog." These sentences incorporate both the smell and sound perceived and the skunk and dog inferred.

---

5 There is a detailed discussion of the conception of sounds as available to the general public in Casey O'Callaghan, "Perception: Auditory," *Stanford Encyclopedia of Philosophy*, 2009.

6 We are also quite happy, of course, to assign acts of perception to animals. I can say not only "Tom saw the dog," but also "The dog saw Tom."

The most important sense for gathering information is the sense of sight and this is the sense on which I shall now concentrate my attention. What are the fundamental perceptions that form the basis for the knowledge acquired through the sense of sight?

4 DIFFERENT EXPRESSIONS OF VISUAL PERCEPTION

When we turn to examine the detailed use of the verbs through which we express visual perceptions, we find an immediate complication. There appear to be two quite different constructions. Usually the verb takes a direct object, e.g. "Tom saw the dog."[7] But there is another common construction in which the verb is followed by a propositional clause, e.g. "Mary saw that the cat was coming into the room." If there are perceptual acts denoted in these two cases, do these perceptual acts have different structures? Does the perceptual act that took place when Tom saw the dog have a simple subject-object structure, Tom being the subject and the dog being the object, whereas in the second case the act has a quite different structure involving a propositional content in much the same way as an act of judgment or a state of belief? It will be a serious complication if we have to postulate two significantly different varieties of perception corresponding to the different idioms.

One very good reason *not* to think that the two different constructions designate two different species of perceptual act is that with a little tweaking it seems that either construction can be legitimately used in each particular case. Instead of saying "Mary saw that the cat was coming into the room," we might equally well say "Mary saw the cat coming into the room."[8] On the other hand, it seems that "Tom saw a dog" can

---

7 For auditory perceptions it is the subject-object construction that is the dominant format. We say we hear either sounds or the things making the sounds. It is with visual perception that the propositional construction finds a natural home – perhaps also tactual perceptions: "I felt that the plate was slipping from my grasp."

8 Barry Stroud, indeed, introduces a special category for this type of expression, which he calls "predicational" seeing. This "is reported in a sentence with a modified noun or noun phrase as complement to the verb 'see.' It involves seeing an object, but the person does not just see an object that, in fact, has a certain property: he sees an object to have a certain property" (*The Quest for Reality*, 102). This distinction would be important for those anxious to unify perception by reducing propositional perception to the perception of some object. It does not worry me, because I am going the other way. "Predicational" seeing, for instance, can be easily assimilated to "propositional" seeing. Seeing the lemon to be yellow is no different from seeing that the lemon is yellow. It is the simple seeing of the lemon that may be harder to handle.

be replaced by "Tom saw that there was a dog in front of him" – if that is where the dog was.

In his recent book Charles Landesman argues, however, that "Tom saw that there was a dog in front of him" and "Tom saw a dog" are not interchangeable.[9] The first "expresses a judgment based upon a visual perception" whereas the second "reports the perception itself" (110). The claim is that the two assertions have different truth conditions. The first would not be true, if because of the poor light, Tom was not sure whether the animal was a cat or a dog, whereas the second would be true, if the animal was in fact a dog, even if Tom did not know that it was a dog. If someone else merely wishes to identify the object perceived by Tom, then it is perfectly proper to use any description which fits that object, even if Tom himself was not in a position to use that description. But if the other person is reporting Tom's *interpretation* of his perception of the object through the use of the propositional construction, there is not the same opportunity for alternative descriptions.

This difference between the two uses of "see" is not actually as cut and dried as Landesman may suppose. Some latitude is permissible even with the propositional construction. When reporting the rescue of my cat, it would seem perfectly proper to say: "The fireman saw that Fluffy was climbing farther up the tree," even although the fireman didn't know that the cat was called Fluffy and couldn't care less! Nevertheless, it would not be proper to say that Tom saw that there was a dog in front of him, if Tom merely saw that there was some creature emerging from the mist, but could not make out what it was.

Such facts about the proper use of certain idioms in the language are very far from proving what Landesman would like to establish. What Landesman would like to show, both here and in an earlier book,[10] is that there are fundamental acts of perception with a subject-object structure, and that based on these are interpretations or judgments to be expressed through the propositional idiom. What is fundamental in visual perception according to Landesman is *seeing things*; once the thing has been seen, judgments can be formed that are to be expressed through the propositional construction. It is possible, however, to offer a very natural account of the widespread use of the idiom exemplified by "Tom saw the dog," which does not suppose that it reveals the primitive phase in perceptual experience. Instead of supposing that the subject-object construction penetrates to what is fundamental in the perceptual

9 *Scepticism: The Central Issues*, 109–10.
10 Charles Landesman, *Color and Consciousness: An Essay in Metaphysics*, chapter 6.

situation, it may be more reasonable to argue that this idiom actually represents a more external and superficial view.

Perhaps it is the propositional construction that reveals the inner structure of acts of perception – the subject-object idiom is used merely for quick identification of the particular act of perception that interests the speaker. This can be done simply by mentioning some object that appears to interest the perceiver, which is much easier to determine than the particular information that the perceiver extracts from the experience.

"Tom saw the dog," for example, can be established with considerable assurance merely by noticing that Tom was looking at the dog. What particular information Tom was extracting from his scrutiny of the dog is harder to determine, and to specify this information through the propositional construction requires a more ambitious claim, which may have greater uncertainty. Perhaps more often than not we make no such ambitious claim and content ourselves with the modest assertion that Tom saw the dog. But this does not mean that we suppose Tom had a visual encounter with the dog in which he extracted no information whatsoever. If through this visual encounter Tom got any information about the dog, however vague, then this information must be expressed through a proposition, so that acts of perception will necessarily involve a propositional component from the very beginning. Any process that may be rightly called a perception must have a propositional structure. The more relaxed truth conditions for the subject-object construction do not have any deep significance, but come from the latitude granted to another person to identify the object associated with Tom's perception in whatever way will best suit the audience, even if that way was not available to Tom himself.

Thus, "Tom saw the dog" indicates that the dog was an object of interest for Tom's visual system; but to unpack the structure of the perceptual act, we must use the more elaborate propositional construction – minimally, "Tom saw that the dog was present," but preferably something more informative, such as "Tom saw that the dog was on the carpet" or "Tom saw that the dog was coming into the room." In other words, it is the propositional form that seems to capture the essence of the complete act of visual perception, whereas the subject-object construction merely identifies one element involved.

This, at any rate, is the view taken by many philosophers – including John Searle.[11] For Searle, perceptions such as visual experiences are

---

11 John R. Searle, *Intentionality*, 40–2.

Intentional states that necessarily involve propositional Intentional content. This content concealed by the subject-object construction is made more explicit by the alternative formulation, e.g. "I have a visual experience (that there is a yellow station wagon there)" (41). One major advantage of this theory is that it solves the notorious problem of how to make the leap from perception to belief. A central function of perception is to provide us with true beliefs about the nature of the world that surrounds us, and in which we have to act. It is easier to explain how we get these beliefs if our theory assumes that some belief is already implicit in the act of perception. The propositional construction is, indeed, essential if we are trying to operate the top-down approach. If we are working back from empirical beliefs that involve inference to their supposed foundations, we must get to perceptions with propositional structure, otherwise we do not have the premises required to found the inferences.

5 CONDITIONS FOR THE USE OF THE PROPOSITIONAL CONSTRUCTION

We have already established in section 3 that the use of verbs of perception such as "smell" and "hear" in ordinary language is not going to draw the line between what is actually perceived and what is merely inferred. We say that we smell the skunk and hear the dog, but the animals are clearly inferred from the smell and the noise. This turns out to be equally true for visual perception. What we quite naturally say that we see will often involve a huge element of inference.

It would be quite natural to say, for instance, that Harry saw that the bridge was about to collapse. But unless we believe in clairvoyance, no perception of the future is thought to be possible. We normally think of perception as a faculty that reveals our immediate environment at the present time. There is, of course, a very simple way to deal with this problem. Why not concede that in this case the construction "Harry saw that p" does not designate an act of perception at all? Instead of saying "Harry saw that the bridge was about to collapse," we might have said "Harry knew that the bridge was about to collapse." This is not a problem, since knowledge of the future is often possible through the use of well-founded inference. Why, then, use the word "see" at all in this case? Obviously, it is to signal that the sense of sight is the important source of evidence for the claim that the bridge was about to give way. What Harry actually saw was no more, say, than that the supports were cracking, which is definitely bad news for anyone crossing the bridge but not the same as an actual vision of its future collapse. My example, then, requires us to break the tie between the legitimate use of the idiom "S sees that *p*" and the existence of an act of visual perception with the propositional content p. Even if we grant, following Searle, that the most explicit formulation of an act of visual perception will be through an expression of the form "S sees that p," the reverse implication cannot be defended. The legitimate use of a sentence in the form "S sees that p" does not prove that an act of visual perception with the propositional content p has taken place.

Let me propose the following analysis as at least a first approximation for the legitimate use of the idiom in the language: "'S sees that p' can be legitimately asserted, if and only if: (1) S believes that p: (2) S's belief that p is based on evidence (information) provided by the sense of sight: (3) p is true." This formula is designed to cover cases where the evidence provided by the sense of sight for S's belief that p *is* just the act of visual perception that p carried out by S, if there are any such cases. But since cases have been found where this is not so, the Trojan horse has been brought within the gates.

Although the third condition I have listed for the correct use of "see" is widely accepted, it has been challenged through counter-examples introduced by Timothy Williamson.[12] What about "Jack saw that the World Bank had agreed to the loan" or "Victor heard that you will be going to Greece next year"? These are perfectly legitimate idioms in the language, and may be legitimately used without any presumption that the embedded proposition is true. Victor really did hear that you will be going to Greece next year, even if this rumour is totally false.

These anomalous cases, however, can be easily neutralized by construing such sentences as essentially elliptical. Jack saw [the report in the paper] that the World Bank had agreed to the loan. Victor heard [the rumour] that you will be going to Greece next year. The propositional clauses are associated, not with the verbs "saw" and "heard," but with the implicit nouns ("report," "rumour"). This explains why the embedded propositions are not necessarily true, since reports may be false and rumours usually are.

The second condition stipulates that the belief involved when we are entitled to say that S sees that p must be *based on* evidence or information provided by the sense of sight. But what counts as "based on"? To say that the belief must be based *exclusively* on evidence provided by sight is impossibly restrictive. When Harry saw that the bridge was about to collapse, the evidence of his eyes provided an important clue, but other information is also required, e.g. about the behaviour of bodies when the

12 Timothy Williamson, *Knowledge and its Limits*, 36–9.

supports are withdrawn. Should we go to the other extreme and say that we can use the verb "see" whenever visual experience makes any contribution whatsoever to the acquisition of knowledge? Sometimes, it seems that we are prepared to go quite far in this direction, but there are limits. I could hardly say that I saw that Fred's car would break down before reaching Vancouver, even if part of my evidence was the way the wheels appeared to wobble as the car made its way along the road! The cut-off point, therefore, must lie somewhere between these extremes. It is not crucial, and not even very valuable, to try to fix it precisely. For one thing, it is unlikely that a clearly demarcated and generally accepted borderline is there to be found.

We are accustomed to use verbs of perception quite generously, even when there is patently a large element of inference involved in reaching the proposition that follows the verb. There is, however, a consideration that restricts our free and easy ways. Once the inferential element is uncovered and explicitly stated, we are no longer entitled to say that we perceived what we originally said we perceived. I may say to the detective investigating a crime: "I saw that John had left the room." On cross-examination, I have to concede that I didn't actually see John passing through the door. I saw that John was in the room, looked away, and when I looked back, he was gone. I inferred that John had left the room, but I didn't actually see him leaving. I must therefore withdraw my original claim that I saw that John had left the room.

In general, although I may very well say that I see that p when I have actually inferred that p, I can no longer *say* that I see that p, once I have explicitly recognized that inference is involved. Once I admit, under pressure, that I have *inferred* that John has left the room, I can no longer claim that I *perceived* this. In ordinary life we use verbs of perception with considerable looseness, because we are normally not that concerned to draw the line between what is actually perceived and what is merely inferred. The interest is focused on the proposition established in the perception, whether it be through direct perception or well-grounded inference. Special concerns are required to change the focus, as in the case where the detective is anxious to establish testimony that will stand up under cross-examination.

The detective will be particularly eager to show that I jumped to the conclusion that John left the room if he has reason to believe that John actually hid behind the sofa when I looked away. If that is so, I did not see that John had left the room, because it is not true that John had left the room. But even if John did leave the room when I thought he did, a detective who is careful to structure his evidence will insist that in this case it is a matter of inference rather than immediate perception. To acknowledge the contribution of inference is important, because it brings the discussion into a public forum. Everyone is on the same footing and can assess whether, given the evidence of my eyes, my conclusion is beyond reasonable doubt. Everyone can consider alternative hypotheses compatible with that evidence, taking them seriously or ruling them out.[13]

I am particularly prepared in this case to concede without a fuss that I did not really see that John had left the room, because I can identify an experience, which I did not have, that would really count as seeing that John had left the room – namely watching him actually passing through the door on his way out. But there are other cases where no such special experience is to be found. Suppose I claim that I saw that the man was drunk, because of the way he was staggering down the street.[14] In my initial response to what I see I might quite naturally say *either* "I saw that the man coming down the street was staggering" *or else* "I saw that the man coming down the street was drunk," since both the embedded propositions are well founded on the evidence of my eyes. The constraint is this: once it is made explicit that what I saw was that the man coming down the street was staggering, I am no longer able to claim that I saw that the man was drunk, even though this would be legitimate enough as a free-standing statement.[15] In this special context, I have to admit that I didn't *see* that the man was drunk – I merely *inferred* this from what I did see. This differs from the case of seeing that John has left the room, because in this case there is no other visual experience providing better evidence that the man was drunk. This is about as good as it gets without a blood test.

Thus, there is a dialectical principle that restricts the use of verbs of perception.[16] In a certain situation, it may be perfectly proper to say

13 There is an example in recent literature where the importance of this kind of articulation forms a central part of the plot. Ian McEwan, in his book *Atonement,* has his character Briony begin by claiming that she *saw* that Robbie was responsible for the attack on Lola and testifying to that effect in court. Although from her point of view, she had every reason to believe that the man was Robbie, she later conceded that she didn't actually see that the man was Robbie, since it was too dark to make out his features for a positive identification. She was assuming that the man must be Robbie for other reasons. She was not lying in court when she said that the man was Robbie, because this she profoundly believed: she misled the court in a more subtle way by claiming that she *saw* that the man was Robbie.

14 I take my example from John R. Searle, *Intentionality,* 76–8. Searle has real difficulty with this case.

15 I am assuming, of course, that the man really was drunk.

16 I call the principle "dialectical," because it restricts, not free-standing statements, but ways in which discourse may be developed.

either "S sees that *p*" or "S sees that *q*," even although *q* has been clearly inferred from *p*. This is because it is legitimate to use verbs of perception even when inference is involved, so long as the belief expressed through this construction is sufficiently founded on the employment of the sense in question. What one cannot do is *say* that inference was involved and continue to claim that one perceived that *p*.

The replacement of a more ambitious claim to see is particularly common in ordinary life when doubts are introduced about the truth of the proposition *p* which forms its content. If doubts are raised about whether the man seen staggering down the street was drunk, I have to withdraw my claim that I saw that he was drunk and retreat to the weaker claim that I saw that he was staggering. It is possible that a man who is staggering may not be drunk and that the stagger may be due to some other cause. Claims to see that *p* must be withdrawn, once doubt is introduced, given that "S sees that *p*" entails "S knows that *p*" and knowledge does not survive in an atmosphere of suspicion. I have conceded that it is perfectly legitimate to *say* "I saw that the man was drunk," so long as I do not bring in the idea that this was inferred from seeing that he was staggering. But although legitimate enough in the context, is it really true? If it were true, how could we be required to correct it?

Should we simply admit that my original claim that I saw that the man was drunk is not true and never was true? It was legitimate to make it before it was explicitly recognized that there was an inference from seeing that the man was staggering, in the sense in which it is sometimes legitimate to make oversimplified and strictly false statements to convey the gist of a matter to a person who is not concerned with absolute precision. It is true that I have come to know that the man is drunk (given that this *was* the reason for the stagger); it is true that my acquisition of this knowledge involves a substantial use of my sense of sight; and the inference from seeing that the man was staggering can easily be ignored until it is explicitly put on the table. Because of the inference involved, my claim to *see* that the man was drunk is strictly false, but people are prepared to let it pass, so long as the existence of the inference is not put under their noses.

This is one way to handle the problem, but there is also an ingenious strategy that will allow us to avoid condemning, as false, claims to see that the man was drunk. The truth of statements made through the use of certain expressions is obviously relative to the rules governing the use of these expressions. Can it both be true that I saw that the man was drunk and false that I saw that the man was drunk, when it is the same visual experience which is described? This is possible only if the rules for the use of this sentence vary with the context of use. The rules change after

it is conceded that I have made an inference. Before the rule change it
was true that I saw that the man was drunk. After the rule change it is not
true that I saw that the man was drunk. There is no question of determining unconditionally whether the statement expressed by the sentence is
true or false without specifying which set of rules is in operation. This
depends on whether or not it is explicitly recognized that I saw that the
man was staggering and inferred that he was drunk. Once the inference
is brought into the picture, the rules for the use of the sentence have to
be tightened. The temptation to allow that I saw that the man was drunk
depends on the looser set of rules, and the competing urge to disallow
this comes from the strict set that denies that it is a case of seeing when
inference has taken place.

6 BASIC ACTS OF VISUAL PERCEPTION

We are now equipped to resume the hunt for the basic acts of perception
that underpin our empirical knowledge of the external world. We have
identified a natural dialectic forming part of ordinary discourse that allows us to withdraw more ambitious claims to perceive when the element
of inference involved has been uncovered. This allows us to work our way
down from what we normally say we perceive until we reach the bedrock
of what we really do perceive in the strictest sense.

The dialectical structure that requires us to modify overenthusiastic
claims to see, when a conspicuous element of inference is explicitly revealed, occurs only sporadically in ordinary life, but the pattern is established, and once established, it can be exploited more extensively and
more systematically than is called for in the ordinary course of events. It
is not difficult to reconstruct many very natural claims to see in order to
expose an element of inference. We may say that Hamlet saw that there
was a man hiding behind the curtain, when all that he really saw was that
the curtain had a suspicious bulge, and the man was inferred as the cause
of this bulge. If the castle at Elsinore had been less well-appointed, and
an economy line of curtaining installed which did not quite reach the
floor, Hamlet, we may say, might have seen that feet were protruding
from underneath the curtain, and inferred the man supported by the
feet. But did Hamlet even see that there were feet? Isn't it true that what
he saw was merely that there were boots, and the feet inside the boots
and the man owning the feet (and the boots) were inferred?

What we have here is a string of empirical beliefs: that there are boots
on the floor; that there are feet protruding from beneath the curtain;
that there is a man behind the curtain. Since each of these beliefs depends largely on the use of the sense of sight, each may legitimately

follow some verb of visual perception. The list is structured in such a way that beliefs that are further along the list are based on, and inferred from, beliefs that are nearer the beginning. The constraint I have identified is that when one proposition in the string is explicitly brought into play, all other propositions inferred from it that are further along the string must be dropped from the list of possible contents for propositional perceptions. What we want to get at is the belief that heads the list from which all the other things we say we see have been inferred.

This belief will be the propositional content of the fundamental act of visual perception which underlies the various things we say we see in ordinary life. This propositional content has to be what it is, no matter what we may choose to *say* that we perceived, incorporating inferred material to a greater or lesser degree. It is perfectly in order for me to say that I saw that the man coming down the street was drunk, until it is pointed out that I saw only that the man was staggering. But since I may have to revise what I say I see, "that the man was drunk" could *never* have been the content of my act of visual perception. To identify the content of the supposed act of visual perception, we must find some proposition q that is such that we could never be required to withdraw the claim that we see that q, because there is some other proposition r from which q has been inferred.

At first sight, the thesis that there is a fundamental proposition defining each perceptual act seems plausible enough. After all, in each example I have used, when the claim to see that p has to be withdrawn, there is always some other proposition q from which p has been inferred. And if we begin to have doubts that q itself may not be entirely free from the taint of inference, then we must posit some other proposition r, constituting the content of the perceptual act, from which q itself has been inferred. Although any specific proposition that is put forward as the content of the perceptual act may be open to challenge, it seems that there must ultimately be *some* propositional content – lurking in the recesses of the mind – that defines the act of perception.

Worry begins, however, when one faces up to the question of where this regress to foundations actually terminates in particular cases. This kind of regress in philosophy is notoriously difficult to stop. To go back to the example of Hamlet and the boots, the dialectic terminated in the claim that Hamlet saw that there were boots. It is clear that this is not the end of the line. From where he was standing, could Hamlet actually see anything more than the front surfaces of the boots? The content of his act of perception will have to be "that there are brown boot-shaped surfaces." Since the concept of a surface presupposes an object of which it is the surface, more generously we might allow that Hamlet saw that there was a pair of objects with brown boot-shaped front surfaces. But this is as far as we can go, since there is a logical gap between objects with boot-shaped front surfaces and real boots. Certainly, there are ostentatious libraries in country houses where the shelves are lined with book facades and not with real books. The visitor may think that he sees that there are books, but the strict content of his act of perception is that there are surfaces resembling the surfaces of the spines of real leather-bound volumes.

To extend the dialectic by replacing "seeing that there are boots" with "seeing that there are surfaces of boots" is not a move likely to be made in ordinary life, but it seems a perfectly legitimate move in the context of the attempt to pin down the precise content of the act of perception. But is this the end of the road? Introducing surfaces does in some degree recognize the influence of perspective in perception, since as we move round the object we see different surfaces (or different parts of the surface) from different points of view. This is not a complete answer, since there is a change in the look of a given surface, such as the top of a table, with a change in the angle from which it is viewed. In any case, there is no recognition so far of the important change that takes place in our act of perception when we change our distance from the object. When we move further away, the information we get about the surface involved will be decreased and this will have a bearing on the propositional content of the act of perception. If he gets far enough away, Hamlet will no longer be able to recognize the surfaces he sees as boot-shaped. Now the change that accompanies my move away from the object changes my information about the relative positions of the object and the perceiver. This means that we must factor into the propositional content of the basic act of perception a specification of our distance to the surface perceived.[17] Since the basic visual act must be concerned, not with a single surface, but with a vast array of interrelated surfaces, its propositional content will have to be extremely complicated. Mere complication is not, of course, a fatal objection in cases like this where we have no basis for assessing what would be *too* complicated, but it certainly undermines the elegance of the initial idea.

There is, however, another difficulty with the attempt to uncover the propositional content of basic perceptual acts. The way the dialectic proceeds is that in order to dethrone one candidate for the position of propositional content, one has to advance the claims of another. To deny

---

17 Strictly, the propositional content must also specify the direction of the surface in question and its orientation with respect to the line of sight.

that Hamlet saw that there were feet protruding from underneath the curtain, we have to insist that Hamlet saw that there were boots. But at the time Hamlet claimed to see that there were feet protruding from underneath the curtain, there is no clear evidence that the concept of boots is present to his mind. And without the presence of this concept, the propositional content that *boots* are protruding from underneath the curtain cannot define a perceptual act. The perceptual act that is supposed to take place cannot have as its content the proposition that there are protruding human feet, because the revised story has shown that the presence of these feet has been inferred. Nor can we assume that it has as its content the proposition that there are protruding *boots*, because there is no clear evidence that the concept of boots is involved in the original perceptual situation.

The essential problem is that the more we do to strip away inferential accretion to reveal, in its purity, the fundamental act of perception, the more necessary it becomes to posit concepts defining the basic perceptual act that do not seem to be involved in the original perceptual situation. Working from the outside, we may claim that a person has not really perceived what he says he has perceived, revealing the required intellectual move through using concepts that were not available to the person at that time. The dilemma is that the basic experience cannot be defined through the concept actually used by the perceiver, since this has been shown to involve a certain element of inference; but on the other hand, the experience is not defined by the concept introduced by the outside observer (Daniel Dennett's *heterophenomenologist*),[18] since this concept is not involved in the actual experience itself.

Thus it appears that the top-down method, instead of reaching bedrock, has disappeared into the sand. One may be reluctant to abandon the theory that there are fundamental perceptual acts involving propositional contents, because it does have one great advantage. The central problem of perception is to explain how subjects attain a coherent knowledge of the world in which they live on the basis of a confused manifold of sensory input. If we are allowed to posit fundamental acts of perception with propositional content at the interface between the two systems, then the move from perception to the tapestry of empirical knowledge becomes intelligible in principle, since the acts of perception will involve empirical knowledge, however primitive. But such a theory is now very difficult to defend.

18 *Consciousness Explained,* 72.

The original reason for introducing acts of perception may have been to find an objective correlate for certain true statements in ordinary language employing verbs of perception. As we have seen, there is a familiar idiom where we say of persons that they perceive that something is the case, e.g. "Tom saw that the cat was coming into the room." We discovered, however, that this statement did not reveal an act of perception with the propositional content that the cat was coming into the room, but rather Tom's *belief* that the cat was coming into the room, acquired on the basis of some use of the sense of sight. That is, the function of this idiom is not to reveal the experiential basis, but to announce the empirical knowledge reached on that basis, together with an indication of the sensory source from which that knowledge has been derived. There is no stipulation whatsoever about the nature of the basis in experience. It is indeed possible that the experiential basis could be an act of perception with *some* propositional content, even if not the complete content embedded in the original statement about what Tom saw, since this clearly involves contributions from other sources. But we ran into serious difficulties trying to specify what these basic acts of perception might be.

Even if we could uncover the basic acts of propositional perception upon which depends the tapestry of empirical knowledge that develops further down the line, we are as far as ever from understanding the connection between fundamental acts of perception that involve cognition and the underlying physiological processes that do not. The propositional theory of perception reduces the gap between empirical knowledge and perceptual experience at the cost of widening the gap between perceptual experience and its causal antecedents.

8

The Search for the Missing Link

1 INTRODUCTION

The problem of perception is to explain how we reach the empirical beliefs that we entertain about the world around us on the basis of the sensory input fed in through the senses. The source of the difficulty is that the outcome of the process is expressed in a discourse using concepts such as belief, truth, reference, and inference, whereas the origination of the process is described in a different discourse using the concepts of natural science, including neurophysiology. In the last chapter we were quite unable to close this gap, whether we began from the bottom up or from the top down.

Thus, it may now be time to consider the alternative suggestion that the experiential basis presupposed in knowledge acquired through perception is not originally organized in propositional form. Using different levels of supplementation and different conceptual resources, we construct on this experiential basis a variety of propositions that form the content of a variety of perceptual beliefs. When the boots of Polonius are visible beneath the curtain, Hamlet may form various beliefs, such as that there are boots beneath the curtain, or that there is a man behind the curtain, or the (erroneous) belief that the King is behind the curtain. If the experiential basis for these beliefs is of a non-propositional kind, how are we to understand this – and how are we to explain the move from this basis to propositional knowledge?

The most promising idea to bridge the gap between the neural processes in the brain and the cognitive life of the experiencing subject is perhaps the introduction of the concept of sensation that appeared in Part One. Sensations can connect the physical and the mental, because they seem to have a foot in both camps. Conceived as *effects* produced in consciousness by the underlying physiological processes, they belong to the causal discourse of natural science (albeit slightly extended). On the other hand, as elements in consciousness they are available as objects for an introspective knowledge that can classify and organize these sensations as successive or co-existent in time.

As we have seen in Part One, the traditional theory of perception, which employs this idea, must collapse. Even if the introduction of sensation as the missing link connecting neural processes and empirical beliefs was on the right track, we cannot explain the acquisition of empirical knowledge in terms of an inference from the sensations to their external causes. Although such inferences are possible, they cannot be primitive, since they presuppose a system of assumptions about a causally organized world of things in space and time that cannot be established through such inferences.

Although we cannot originally reach the things in the external world by an *inference* from the sensations produced in us, perhaps our original empirical beliefs are *generated* by these sensations in some other way. "Somehow or other" there is a transition from sensations in us to a knowledge of an external world. The task of the philosophy of perception is to explain in detail how this transition may take place.

The key move may be to recognize that there is more to the items we have been calling sensations than the traditional theory has been prepared to allow. For the purposes of the traditional theory, it was sufficient to conceive the sense experiences at the interface between the physiological and the cognitive as mere sensations, mere effects of the external causes, since the function of these items is to be put to work in inferences from the character of the effects to the character of their external causes. Perhaps this is a much reduced vision of the true character of these items and we may require a richer conception.

I originally selected the term "sensation" for two reasons. Partly, I am relying on the authority of Immanuel Kant, who introduces "sensation" (Latin *sensatio*) as a technical term to designate "The effect of an object upon the faculty of representation."[1] This is quite close to Hume's term "impression," once one strips away the metaphor of the seal impressing its form upon the *tabula rasa*, the blank tablet of the mind. My other reason is to exploit the comparison with the sensations of pain that are sometimes produced in us by the impact of external things. This is a very old argument that Berkeley, for instance, introduced near the beginning of the first of his *Three Dialogues between Hylas and Philonous*. Berkeley compares the heat that we think we perceive as a quality of the

---

1 Immanuel Kant, *Critique of Pure Reason*, translated by Norman Kemp Smith, A20 B34.

object to the sensation of pain we experience when the heat is intensi-
fied. His conclusion is that the heat that is directly perceived must also
be a sensation.

This comparison with pains can be extended with some plausibility
to tastes and smells, interpreting the sweet taste as a sensation produced
in us by the sugar and the unpleasant smell as a sensation produced in us
by the skunk. The notion that the sounds we hear can be understood as
auditory sensations is more problematic.[2] By the time we get to the sense
of sight, talk about visual sensations, although not impossible, begins to
look forced and artificial.

Perhaps we can find another way to describe those inner items – formerly known as sensations – that are present in visual experience. This
alternative description might allow us to give due weight to the considerable differences between sensations in the ordinary sense, like pains, and
whatever is immediately present in visual experience. Although in ordinary discourse we use the word "sensation" to describe things like pains
and tickles, we do not normally talk about visual sensations.

The hope is that a fresh conceptualization of the inner items may
dissolve the barrier through which the sensations block access to the
external world that we must somehow reach for genuine empirical
knowledge. If the sensations produced through sensory stimulation are
distinct existences (in Hume's sense), the external objects responsible
could be reached only by causal argument, which, as we have seen, is an
operation not permitted at the beginning of our cognitive life. One
promising suggestion is to treat the inner items in visual experience,
not as sensations, but as appearances.

2 APPEARANCES

In ordinary life, we do not talk about visual sensations; instead, we talk
about how things *look* or *appear*. It is universally accepted that how a certain tree will look to me will change when I change my position relative
to the tree. This is equivalent to the technical doctrine that the visual
sensation produced by the tree will vary with the relative positions of the
tree and the observer. Just as the sensations produced in me by an external object are a function of the object itself and the conditions of observation constituting the causal chain connecting the object to the mind,

2 See, for instance, Casey O'Callaghan, "Auditory Perception," *Stanford Encyclopedia of
Philosophy*, 2.1.1.

so also how the object appears to me is a function of that object itself, together with these same conditions of observation.

The theory of appearing has the advantage of enlisting the ways that we talk in ordinary language about many items classed as sensations in the traditional philosophical theory. This theory has been widely adopted in recent years, with R.M. Chisholm as one of its leading proponents.[3] According to this theory, what I have been calling sensations are not to be considered inner objects of cognition at all, but rather the ways in which external objects appear to a subject. The essential feature of the traditional theory that the theory of appearing seeks to replace was to identify sensations as the original objects of cognition. This was thought to be a mistake, since the sensations are not objects in their own right, but appearances of reality. The fundamental assumption made by the classical theory is that our original cognition has a two-term subject-object structure. The cognitive subject makes judgments through conceptualizing objects of awareness. This account of cognitive structure is taken over directly from the naive realism of common sense, substituting internal objects – the sensations – for external objects. We normally think of ourselves as aware of ordinary physical objects, like tables and chairs, which we describe in empirical judgments. The traditional theory brings the objects of awareness inside the mind, and the external domain drops away. But there is no guarantee that this familiar two-term analysis of cognitive structure must be correct.

The theory of appearing suggests a three-term analysis for the basic cognitive fact. There is the experiencing subject; there is the object of experience; and there is how the object appears to the subject. For example, when I look at a table, there is myself as cognitive subject; there is the table I am looking at; and there is how the table looks to me. This more complex theory finds a place for all the elements that must be recognized in the experiential situation. The alternative two-term theories both leave out an important element. Naive realism has no place for that element in experience that is a function of the conditions of observation. The fatal flaw in the traditional theory is that it can find no place for external objects beyond the sensory content.

The mere proposal of a three-term analysis for the fundamental cognitive state is not in itself a conclusive answer to the determined sceptic. We may agree with Kant about the absurdity of the "conclusion that there can be appearances without something which appears."[4] But how can we be

---

3 R.M. Chisholm, "The Theory of Appearing," *Philosophical Analysis*, ed. Max Black, 102–18.

4 *Critique of Pure Reason*, translated by Norman Kemp Smith, B xxvii.

sure that what we are calling appearances are legitimately conceptualized in this way? After all, if we also accept Kant's definition of the sensation as the effect of the object, the existence of the sensation will entail the existence of its external cause. Every *effect* must have a cause. The crucial question is whether sense-data are sensations in this sense. In the same way, the crucial question is whether sense-data are appearances, with everything this entails. The suggested analysis is a proposal that may be mistaken; it is *possible* that the subject is directly aware of sense-data without a path to move beyond. The whole point of introducing the concept of sense-data at the beginning of the last century was to block the automatic positing of the causes of sensations and the things which appear.

The trouble is that although the theory of appearing assumes the possibility of a direct cognitive contact with the physical world, it does not make this possibility any more intelligible than did its predecessor, naive realist theory. Nicolas Malebranche would still have his worries about how we can get at the external objects when the soul has no capacity to walk among the stars.[5] The theory of appearing improves on naive realism because it finds a place for the variations in experience with changing conditions of observation; but it does nothing to resolve the fundamental difficulty.

Another problem with the notion of appearance is that it is an isolated concept without much connection to other systems. How can we describe the relation between appearance and reality except by saying that the appearances are the ways the reality appears? An alternative conceptualization of these items as sensations introduces a much richer web. The relation between the appearance and the object is of a mysterious *sui generis* kind; the relation between the sensation and the object is the familiar causal relation that applies throughout the universe. It is acknowledged that how an object appears to me is a function of the thing itself, together with the conditions of observation. But how can we understand this, unless the appearance is an effect produced through the chain of causes and effects determined by the conditions of observation, in which case the appearance *is* a sensation? The reduction of how things appear to the sensations they produce also has the advantage mentioned before of incorporating the ways things appear in sense experience in a much wider class of phenomena. We can integrate in the same class the sensation of pain induced by the bite of a mosquito with the sensation of sound produced by its ominous whine, if we are prepared to recognize how the mosquito sounds as an auditory sensation induced by the sound waves it emits.

5 See chapter 1, note 9.

3 JOHN MCDOWELL

With the collapse of the theory of appearing back into the framework provided by the standard causal theory, we again face the problem of explaining the transition from the causal to the cognitive. The seriousness of this problem is clearly recognized by John McDowell in his book *Mind and World.* McDowell brings the problem into focus by using a notion of "the space of concepts," which is "at least part of what Wilfrid Sellars calls 'the space of reasons'"[6] (5). The space of concepts covers the traditional domain of philosophical logic, incorporating concepts, judgments, and inferences. Judgments and beliefs involve concepts and one judgment is derived from another judgment as a conclusion justified by its premise. This space of concepts is the domain of the understanding.

The trouble is that although the understanding, at least according to Kant, has a certain spontaneity, it cannot be allowed to operate entirely free from all constraint. As McDowell points out, "if our freedom in empirical thinking is total, in particular if it is not constrained from outside the conceptual sphere, that can seem to threaten the very possibility that judgments of experience might be grounded in a way that relates them to a reality external to thought" (5). Within the space of reasons there is no explanation of how a judgment can be generated by what McDowell called "a brute impact from the exterior" (8). From the other side, there is no explanation of how a physical process can produce anything but another physical process. The notion of justification keeps us within the space of reasons; the notion of cause and effect confines us to the domain of nature. Our problem arises at the interface between these two systems. We are back again, it seems, to the original position that somehow or other we begin to operate with judgments in the space of reasons on the basis of a sensory input organized in a causal fashion without being able to explain how, precisely, the transition takes place.

In the preceding chapter I explained how what we say we perceive when we talk to other people usually goes well beyond the revised claim we would make if asked to be more cautious. I say I hear a dog, when I really hear only a barking noise. Hearing the barking noise, combined with other assumptions, provides a justification for the claim to hear the dog. This suggests the possibility of the top-down approach, in which we attempt to uncover the basic acts of perception that the more ambitious claims to perceive that we make in ordinary life depend on. Unfortunately, as we discovered, the top-down approach disappears into the sand,

---

6 I have already introduced the space of reasons in chapter 2, section 2.

instead of reaching the bedrock foundation we are seeking. Nevertheless, the string of claims to perceive – ranging from the cautious to the more dubious – must surely have some foundation in experience, if these claims are not to be entirely arbitrary. The problem is to explain the connection between the empirical belief and its foundation in experience.

John McDowell denies that the first step on the way to our familiar empirical knowledge could be "a move from an impression, conceived as the bare reception of a piece of the Given, to a judgement justified by the impression" (9). He claims, on the contrary, that any justification of empirical judgments must take place within a space of reasons where concepts are necessarily involved. The central position in this argument is occupied by the notion of *justification*. The more cautious claims to perceive identified in the top-down approach provide some level of justification for the more ambitious claims. Moreover, the empirical beliefs reached through perception may be confirmed and justified by further observations, using the same or different senses. I can verify my claim that the cat is on the mat, by taking another, closer, look, or by reaching out to touch it. When I bring my sense of touch into play, I confirm my claim to see that the cat is on the mat through a rational relation[7] between a proposition backed by the sense of touch and a proposition backed by the sense of sight.

The central puzzle in the philosophy of perception, however, is not how one observational statement can provide at least a partial justification for another. It concerns the relationship between the sense experiences that provide the backing for our empirical beliefs and the empirical beliefs based upon these sense experiences. McDowell's contention is that if we take the sense experiences to justify the beliefs, we are operating within the space of reasons. "Empirical justifications depend on rational relations, relations within the space of reasons" (6). This means that we cannot treat the sense experiences as mere given impressions or sensations. For McDowell "When we trace the ground for an empirical judgement, the last step takes us to experiences. Experiences already have conceptual content, so this last step does not take us outside the space of concepts" (10).

McDowell does indeed concede that the picture he is anxious to displace can exempt us from blame. We cannot be accused of adopting our empirical beliefs through an arbitrary exercise of our spontaneity, since the picture traces these beliefs to "a brute impact from the exterior" (8).

---

7 The rational relation here is not, of course, logical entailment, but a form of support and confirmation, in that it eliminates the risk of hallucination or a visual illusion generated by a stage magician or experimental psychologist.

We do not bear the responsibility, since we are subjected to causal forces beyond our control. The trouble is that this picture "offers exculpations where we wanted justifications"[8] (8).

It is certainly not out of order to seek justifications for our empirical beliefs, especially when we have our doubts. One way, as we have seen, is to make further observations and use the results of these observations to support the original belief. But another way is to recollect or re-enact the sense experience that was responsible for the belief in question, provide a careful and precise description of that experience, and then argue that the only reasonable causal explanation of the experience is the state of affairs affirmed by the empirical belief. This style of justification will, indeed, use concepts in the description of the experience (not to mention the complicated causal argument that is required). But it does not presuppose that these concepts, or any concepts, are built into the sense experience itself.[9] This kind of justification works well enough even if the sense experiences are reduced to mere impressions or sensations – the effects of the external causes upon the mind.

To give an example, when I look at my desk, I enjoy an image in the centre of my visual field produced by light reflected from the surface of the desk. If I recognize that this kind of visual image is typically generated by the surface of a desk and that there is nothing atypical about the situation, I am entitled to infer that there is indeed a desk in front of me. My claim to see that there is such a desk in front of my eyes has been given a justification, whether it needs it or not.

This justification takes place completely within the space of reasons as defined by Sellars and McDowell, utilizing concepts, judgments, and inferences. This kind of justification, however, can take place only *after* the

---

8 McDowell's argument is curiously reminiscent of the position advanced by the late-nineteenth- century idealist F.H. Bradley in Note A to the second edition of *Appearance and Reality*. "Thought demands to go *proprio motu*, or, what is the same thing, with a ground and a reason. Now, to pass from A to B, if the ground remains external, is for thought to pass with no ground at all," 501.

9 We may offer a justification for Hamlet's belief that there were feet protruding from underneath the curtain by asserting that Hamlet experienced a boot-shaped visual image, although we have no reason to suppose that Hamlet's visual experience involved the concept of "boots," or any other concept. Concepts come in when we describe the image experienced as "boot-shaped" in providing a *justification* for Hamlet's belief, using, of course, the additional premise that boots usually encase feet. Gareth Evans makes a related point when he denies "that only those information-bearing aspects of the sensory input for which the subject has concepts can figure in a report of his experience." "It is not necessary, for example," he goes on to say, "that the subject possess the egocentric *concept* 'to the right' if he is to be able to have the experience of a sound as being to the right." *The Varieties of Reference*, 159.

original empirical belief has already formed on the basis of the sense experience. One cannot talk about justification, unless the belief to be justified is already on the table. Not that one is necessarily committed to this belief; indeed, a search for justification is usually undertaken only when there is some doubt. But the proposition to be justified has to already be in play.

This is why I called this kind of operation a "second pass" in chapter 2, section 2. I argued that this kind of justification for empirical beliefs was legitimate enough (that is why the traditional theory of perception has its appeal); but it could not reproduce the process by which our empirical beliefs are originally acquired on the basis of sense experience, since it is a sophisticated maneuver only possible after we have built up our empirical knowledge of the physical world as a causal system.

A second pass can therefore provide a justification for our empirical beliefs by supplying judgments about our sense experiences. This is a justification in the strict sense, because we have one judgment supported by another judgment through the use of causal reasoning. This justification, however, begins with a classification or conceptual description of particular sensations or sense experiences, necessary to form the judgment that can function as a premise in a justification. This may be a problem, if it is attempted by a sense-datum theory as the first stage in our construction of empirical knowledge. But when we are justifying empirical beliefs through an examination of sense experience on a second pass, we undertake this task only after we have already built up the cognitive resources necessary to make empirical judgments about external objects.

However that may be, it is clear that McDowell would remain deeply unsatisfied. Even if he accepts my story that there is a way to justify judgments about the external world by introducing judgments about sense experiences, he would argue that the essential problem has merely been postponed, but not solved. The new problem is: "How can we make judgements about our own sense experiences, about our own inner life?" McDowell is happy to concede that judgments are possible within the domain which Kant calls "inner sense." "The realm of thought and judgement includes judgements about the thinker's own perceptions, thought, sensations and the like" (18). For McDowell, however, the problem of judgment is a general problem that must be faced whether the judgment concerns external objects or inner states. Any judgment is an act of the mind and an exercise of spontaneity. The recognition of this may "generate the spectre of a frictionless spinning in the void" (18). Even the conceptualization of given sensations involved in a judgment about them faces a systematic difficulty. The conceptualization cannot be arbitrary: apart from some constraint, the judgment will not be entitled to make a claim to truth. The problem is that "a bare presence cannot supply a justificatory input into a conceptual repertoire from outside it" (20). A sensation must somehow justify whatever concepts are applied to it, or else the judgments about it are arbitrary; on the other hand, there is no question of justification unless the sensation is construed as an experience involving a conceptual element.

It looks as if we have made no progress towards cracking the nut. Judgments require justification, whether the topic is an external object or an internal sensation. It is not entirely true, however, that the situation is unaltered and that the introduction of the second pass has changed nothing. We know very well that we can make mistakes about the external world, sometimes expensive mistakes. Therefore, it can be perfectly natural, when we have our doubts, to look for a justification for empirical beliefs to avoid the expensive mistakes. This justification will take the form of other judgments, sometimes based on the evidence of other senses, but sometimes involving an attempt to characterize the original sense experiences associated with the beliefs in question.

The notion of justification that I have been explaining is, I believe, reasonably well defined, but does it continue to make sense when it is transferred to descriptions of sensations or sense experiences? Looking for other judgments that support and justify my judgments about my inner states is not something I find myself doing in the natural course of events, and it is not even something that I can push myself to do in the service of a philosophical theory. It is not that I get only one chance to describe my inner life and that what I say about my inner states is incorrigible. I must surely be given the opportunity to submit a new, improved description. My point is that the structure of justification operating in connection with beliefs about the external world does not appear to have an application to the inner domain.

Be that as it may, McDowell does have a point. There must be something about our sense experiences that makes one classification appropriate and another inappropriate, one description correct and another incorrect. One might even get away with saying that the application of one concept is justified and the application of another unjustified. The mistake is to slide into saying that a correct description has a justification, because this is to suggest that there is some other proposition justifying it. This, in turn, entails that the justification must have conceptual content, since every proposition necessarily involves the application of some concept.

Even if I am right in suggesting that McDowell is misusing the notion of justification by extending its application beyond the cases where it can be comfortably employed, McDowell may also be right in suggesting that anything correctly described as sense experience necessarily involves a conceptual element. This is a matter still to be settled, which we shall consider at a later point. However, if sense experience is to be brought within the space of reasons by recognizing its conceptual component, we have merely shifted the boundary line, but not removed the fundamental gap between the space of reasons and the space of nature. In the next section I shall try to unite the two sides of this divide by exploiting the concept of *information*. The description of sensory input as "a brute impact from the exterior" seems unduly harsh. Perhaps the gap between input and cognition can be reduced if we think of the sensory input as the bearer of information.

4 INFORMATION

At the conscious and cognitive level we believe we have information about the environment that we can use to guide our behaviour. This information, we also believe, has been transmitted to our sensory systems and brains from the external objects by purely physical and causal processes in which the pattern of information is preserved in spite of transformations required by the nature of the vehicle. There is transmission of information when a physical state contains information that was present in its causal antecedents. For example, the rings on the stump of a tree preserve information about the history of the tree during its formative years. Our various sensory systems have been crafted by nature for the rapid and efficient transmission of information about what is important in our environment. We have also devised, especially in recent years, ingenious communication systems for the transfer and processing of information, culminating in digitalization. These systems for the propagation of information are all completely causal in character.

The concept of sensation in its philosophical use is formed when we imagine the extension into the mind of the standard causal system for the transfer of information. The notion of sensation is introduced when we think of the transmission of this information to the mind through the sensory systems. These sensations contain information transmitted from the environment that has produced them, and so represent that environment in the same way as the rings on a tree represent its history. We are conceiving the sensations as states of mind containing information that can be transmitted further down the line, in the way in which Hume envisages the derivation of ideas from impressions. This account seems inevitable in order to explain how the required information about the world gets into the mind. But once the information has arrived, what are we to do with it? There is no automatic mechanism to promote a mere sensation into a cognition. And if we introduce cognition *of* the sensations, we fall once again into the discredited sense-datum theory. We are still as far as ever from explaining how sense experience, with its causal connection to its physiological antecedents, can be the basis for an empirical knowledge of the external world.

What we need to do is to assign to the experiencing subject a capacity to *extract* the information from the manifold of sensory input. It is not enough for the subject to receive and transmit the information. After all, this is no more than a radio can do, with its receiver for radio waves and its loudspeaker for transmitting sound waves. This extraction of information from what is fed into the system is the very essence of the cognitive life.

In his book *The Conscious Mind*, David Chalmers brings the concept of information to centre stage as the key to connecting the mental and the physical.[10] There is an intelligible connection because the very same information can have both a physical and a phenomenal realization. Chalmers did not, however, posit the extraction of information as distinct from its mere transmission. He believed at the time that intentional states like belief could be explained as functional states and that it was the phenomenal reality of our experiential states that posed what he called "the hard problem." This means that he can work with the simpler notion that experiential states such as sensations merely reproduce in a new arena the information being fed in through the sensory system.

If one abandons the functional explanation of cognitive states to which Chalmers subscribed, one requires a much more radical distinction between the realization of information in mental and physical systems. The information in physical systems is available for transmission, but the information in the mind has been extracted to constitute beliefs and other cognitive states. This reveals, indeed, the essential difference between a mind and a computer. Although a computer has an unrivaled capacity for transmitting and processing information, it is quite unable to *extract* any information from the masses of data passing through it. Indeed, what passes through the computer can be given the honorific title of information, only by reference to the human capacity to *extract* meaningful information from what emerges when the computer has done its work.

10 I provide more detail about the concept of information that Chalmers employs in an earlier work, *Why Consciousness Is Reality*, chapter 7.

The concept of the extraction of information that I feel obliged to use is, of course, a very special idea, like the idea of cognition itself. The notion is useful, because we seem to have some intuitive understanding of what it involves. We know roughly what we mean when we say that knowledge of the tree's history requires a scientist to extract the information contained in the tree rings – but what more can we say about what is going on when this extraction of information takes place?

The central point is that the extraction of information is an act that must be performed by a unitary subject. The systems that contain the information to be extracted do not require this kind of unity. The information is transmitted to the brain by a variety of sensory systems dispersed throughout the body. Even the brain itself, whose activity seems to be the last stage before the extraction of information, does not have the necessary tight unity, since it is an immense swarm of interconnected neurons.

The second point is that the information extracted must inform about something. The obvious supposition is that the information informs about the state of the brain from whose activity it has been extracted. This is a crucial error. Although the information has been extracted from the activity in the brain, the information encoded in the brain is not specifically information about the present condition of the brain, since according to the theory it is the very same information that has been transmitted through the stimulation of the sensory systems.

It would be most satisfactory if the information extracted from the activity in the brain could be taken as information about the things in the external world from which this information was originally transmitted. Through the sense of sight, for instance, we get information about visible objects nearby, where the information is transmitted through the pattern of light waves reflected from their surfaces. It is these objects that are important to us and figure in our plans for the future. Reference to an external domain is somehow built into the act of extracting information from the flow of sensory stimulation, which is the basis for empirical knowledge. We use the information to characterize the things in the external world in accordance with interests that are, in the beginning, of a very practical nature. We are, of course, still very far from explaining how all this is possible. Nevertheless, it looks as if the notion of information may supply the missing link between the physical and the cognitive – between the space of nature and the space of reasons – if we are able to make a radical distinction between the *extraction* of information and its mere *transmission* in physical systems.

5 THE ANALOGY WITH UNDERSTANDING LANGUAGE

Perhaps it may be useful to compare the extraction of information from sensory input with the extraction of information from what is said to us or written down in a language we understand. Linguistic expressions are conventional signs used in a society to express a meaning that a speaker or writer wishes to convey. Other people can then decode the meaning of the signs to extract the information they contain. In the same way, one may suppose, the perceiver decodes the meaning of the natural signs provided by the sensory input to extract information about the world. Since the extraction of information from linguistic expressions is not a simple causal process, but a matter of understanding what is said or written through familiarity with the language used, the comparison of perception with linguistic understanding allows us to claim that the extraction of information in perception is not a simple causal process either.

The analogy between perceptual experience and the understanding of language had some currency in the early modern period. An explicit statement is to be found in Charles Bonnet, *Essai de Psychologie*: "What a word is to an idea which it represents, motion is, so to speak, to perceptions which it causes. It is a kind of sign used by the CREATOR to arouse in the Soul, a certain perception, and to arouse there only that perception."[11] According to John Yolton, traces of this kind of view are to be found even in Descartes himself. He quotes a passage from *Le Monde*: "But, if words, which signify nothing except by the convention of men, are sufficient to make us conceive of things with which they have no resemblance, why is Nature not able to have also established a certain sign which makes us have the sensation of light, even though this sign has no feature which is similar to that sensation."[12]

The case where we acquire information through understanding linguistic expressions is illuminating, because it gives us an example where there is clearly an extraction of information which is very different from the transmission of information from one physical system to another. The information can be extracted only by those who understand the language used. But this special case does nothing to make intelligible the process of perception. The reason we can extract information when we read a book is because the information has been put into print by the

11 Leyden: E. Luzac, 1754. Quoted by John W. Yolton, *Perceptual Acquaintance from Descartes to Reid*, 29.

12 Translated and quoted by John W. Yolton, *Perception and Reality*, 186.

author of the book, using the agreed conventions of a language we understand. We are extracting, from the book, information that has already been extracted by its author, so that it can be conveyed to others through the use of a system of signs.[13] There is no comparable explanation of the extraction of information from the sensory input, unless we are prepared to bring in the Author of Nature. This move was more congenial to philosophers in the seventeenth century than it is today.

13 The use of signs for the exchange of information among cognitive subjects is a complex issue well beyond the scope of this work. I am confining myself to the original extraction of information in perception that is required to provide what I can exchange with others. It is certainly possible that the discussion of the procedures through which we exchange information with our fellows might throw some light on the processes through which we originally extract this information. My suspicion, however, is that things are the other way round: a theory of signs must be based on a solid understanding of how we originally acquire the information we symbolize.

9

The Nature of Sense Experience

1 THE TWO FACES OF SENSE EXPERIENCE

In the effort to connect the physiological processes that convey information from the external world with the state of mind that constitutes knowledge of that external world, the notion of sense experience is the key idea. In order to perform this linking function sense experience must have two faces. It must face up to serve as the ground for the empirical knowledge that is based upon it. It must face down in order to receive the input from the physiological states immediately responsible for its content. The problem is to understand how the same thing can have two faces. Janus, the Roman god of doorways, did have two faces, looking into the past and the future, but Janus is a mythical being.

The traditional causal representative theory of perception had a neat way to handle the difficulty by distinguishing between sensations proper, which are mere effects of the sensory input, and judgments describing the given sensations, which supply the foundations for our empirical knowledge. Unfortunately, this celebrated theory has other sins, and cannot account for the original acquisition of knowledge about the world.[1] Perhaps the solution is to argue that the very same state may be conceptualized in two different ways. The sense experience can be regarded as a simple effect of antecedent causes, in which case it is called "sensation." The very same sense experience can also be regarded as a cognitive state, functioning in the space of reasons to ground our empirical beliefs, in which case it is called "perception."

This distinction helps us to resolve a certain ambivalence in our conception of sensation. On the one hand, we tend to think of a sensation as a distinct existence with a causal link to the object with which it is

---

1 See chapter 1.

correlated. This was certainly the way David Hume was thinking in the *Treatise* when he affirmed that all our impressions are distinct existences: he is using the word "impression" to emphasize the causal link to the impressing object. But on the other hand, we find it difficult to believe that sensations can survive apart from the rich complex of experience surrounding the conscious subject. The solution is to say that the concept of sensation has been constructed by abstraction from the sense experience we enjoy. Because it has been abstracted, it can be treated as a distinct existence with merely causal relations to other entities; but because it has been abstracted, we cannot entirely forget its original setting.

Kant draws a very similar distinction in an important passage in the *Critique of Pure Reason*, in which he gives his official taxonomy for the genus *representation* (*repraesentatio*) (A 320 B 376–7). Although he seems to allow for purely mechanical representation, when a physical state preserves the same information as the state that it represents, the focus of his attention is on conscious representation which, following Leibniz, he calls *perception*.[2] He then goes on to make an extremely interesting distinction. "A *perception* which relates solely to the subject as a modification of its state is *sensation* (*sensatio*), an objective perception is *knowledge* (*cognitio*)" (A 320 B 376–7).

Does this mean that Kant believes that there are two distinct species of perceptions – sensations *and* cognitions?[3] Are some of our perceptions cognitions proper whereas others are mere sensations? Does experience begin in sensation and then through processes too arcane to be clearly explained emerge at the level of perceptual knowledge? It is more plausible to think of Kant as accepting a single set of perceptions, which can be considered in different ways. This is confirmed by his original definition of sensation at the beginning of the Transcendental Aesthetic: "The effect of an object upon the faculty of representation, so far as we are affected by it, is *sensation*" (A 19-20 B 34). What is the point of the qualification "so far as we are affected by it"? Why not just say: "The effect of an object upon the faculty of representation IS *sensation*"? The introduction of the clause "so far as we are affected by it" must be connected with the later statement that a sensation "relates solely to the subject as the modification of its state."

I would like to think that the passages I have quoted allow me to enroll Kant in support of the distinction I have drawn between sensation and

---

2 This sense of perception that embraces sensation is, of course, a wider sense than the sense in which I have contrasted perception with sensation.

3 I change the word "knowledge" in Norman Kemp Smith's translation to "cognition" to keep closer to the Latin technical term Kant had in mind.

perception, although I have to admit that the basis in Kant's writing is suggestive rather than secure. In any event, with or without Kant I have introduced a distinction to explain how it is possible for sense experience to have two faces, so that we can distinguish sensation from objective perception. We are still a long way, however, from understanding how the two aspects of sense experience can be integrated together. On the one hand, we tend to think of a sense experience as a distinct existence with a merely causal link to its antecedent conditions; on the other hand, we find it difficult to believe that sense experiences can be boiled down to sensations conceived as the mere effects of external causes. This resistance may explain the attraction of the theory of appearances discussed in chapter 8, section 2. I pushed this theory to the side on the ground that the appearances are functions of the external objects together with the conditions of observation and are therefore just sensations. The objection evaporates, however, if the theory of appearance does not purport to introduce entities distinct from sensations, but is an alternative way of describing the very same sense experiences, also known as sensations. This alternative conceptualization has the advantage of offering some explanation of how sense experience can provide a foundation for empirical knowledge. The way that the tree appears to me provides some justification for my belief about what the tree really is, so long as I make suitable allowances for the perspective and any special conditions of observation. This is promising, but the problem is far from completely solved. It remains a mystery how the same entity can be regarded in one conceptualization as an appearance and in another as a sensation. How can the ways things appear to us be considered as effects of physical causes?

The mystery is perhaps connected with the isolation of the conceptual scheme associated with the theory of appearing, to which I have already referred. This scheme of concepts is derived from a fragment of ordinary language that does, indeed, have a legitimate use, but whose interface with other conceptual schemes is not well defined. We must therefore try to integrate the concept of appearance in a wider scheme.

The constraints that we must satisfy are that sense experience must both be the outcome of a causal process and at the same time a cognitive state. It must be the outcome of a causal process, since its content is a function of a chain of causes and effects determined by the object and the conditions of observation, including the condition of the sensory apparatus. But sense experience is also considered the very foundation of our empirical knowledge and it is difficult to understand how this can be the case unless sense experience is itself a kind of cognition, and not mere sensation.

Thus, we can consider a perception solely as it relates to the subject as the modification of its state, as a mere effect of the object upon the faculty of representation, and call it "sensation." Alternatively, we can consider this perception as a foundation for empirical knowledge and call it "cognition."[4] But how can we make these two aspects of perception cohere together? To answer this question is to bridge the gap that separates the cognitive and the causal – a gap whose existence constitutes the very centre of the problem of perception!

2 SENSE EXPERIENCE AS RESPONSE

The dilemma is that we must regard sense experience as both the outcome of a causal process and the ground for empirical knowledge. This was the essence of the problem that worried John McDowell. How could a brute impact from the exterior provide a justification for our beliefs about the world? The rhetoric may appear to carry the point, but it is soundly based on the standard idea of causal connection. This is no more than the idea that events of type B follow events of type A in accordance with a regular law. No account is offered to explain why the law must be obeyed. There is no explanation of how the cause determines its effect in the way it does. There is a vision of the universe as governed by causal law, and we make no attempt to probe more deeply to explain how this is possible. We simply use the regularities we notice to predict the future.

Perhaps the time has now come to crack open the concept of causality and get inside the hard smooth shell it normally offers to our view. If we are forced to recognize sense experience as an effect of antecedent physiological processes, perhaps we can reconcile this and the role sense experience has in the grounding of empirical knowledge by looking more deeply into what it is for something to be an effect, at least in this special case. We may discover that the effect produced in consciousness by the external world is very far from being a "brute impact from the exterior."

The key move is to conceive the sense experience as the *response* of the perceiving subject to the incoming stimulus. Given that a subject will tend to respond in the same way to the same sort of stimulus, this will preserve the regularity we need for causal connection. We may not be able to enforce the complete and total regularity required by classical determinism,

4 In calling sense experience the foundation for empirical knowledge, I am leaving entirely open the question of what more may be required, if anything, to move from sense experience to empirical knowledge proper, such as the function of the understanding with its Kantian concept of the object in general.

but this may be a good thing.[5] There is certainly sufficient regularity for us to think of the sense experience as the effect of external causes.

To make this solution work, it is necessary to give the term "response" its full meaning. Classical behaviourists, such as J.B. Watson and B.F. Skinner, also gave the notions of stimulus and response a central role in their system, but their concept of response was very much a stripped-down version. For them, the response to the stimulus was a purely causal and mechanical outcome, and was a function of the nature of the stimulus and the state of the system. The original concept of a response, however, is the concept of a kind of action. Narrowly, it is the verbal answer that a person gives to a question which has been asked. More broadly, it is any reaction of the subject to a given situation that requires attention and must be handled by the subject in an appropriate way.

The concept of a response in this rich sense is absolutely central, because of the way it combines aspects of the active and the passive. In its active dimension the response that is sense experience is a creation of the subject. It is in fact an act of self-creation insofar as the sense experience created is not detached from the subject, but constitutes in part the character of that subject. But sense experience is not a creation out of nothing – it has a passive as well as an active dimension. As well as being an act of the subject, sense experience conforms to antecedent physical processes. The construction of sense experience is an act that involves an appropriate response to the sensory input.

This notion of response requires a radical revision in the standard concept of cause and effect. We normally think of an effect as the *passive* outcome of the activity of the cause, such that the character of the effect is completely determined by that cause. We must now move the activity to the effect. We must change from the picture of the present compelling the future to a picture of the present incorporating the past. The causal relation between the unified experiencing subject and the manifold of physical processes that contribute the input must be understood in a radically new way. The subject somehow combines a given manifold in a single unified whole. There is an act of combination through which are brought together the contributions of the various senses and the manifold of information within each sensory modality.[6]

5 I discuss this question in *Why Consciousness Is Reality*, chapter 3.

6 This account of causal connection is very close to the theory proposed by A.N. Whitehead in *Process and Reality*. I give a brief account of Whitehead's theory in *Why Consciousness Is Reality*, chapter 9, section 3. Whitehead intends his theory to apply to all cases of causal connection throughout the universe; I introduce my theory to explain the extraction of information by the conscious subject. It may or may not have a wider application.

If we go back to the discussion of information in the previous chapter (section 4), the enjoyment of sense experience may be considered the extraction of information transmitted through the sensory system. If the extraction of information is in essence an act performed by a cognitive subject, this will mean that sense experiences belong to our cognitive life and form part of the space of reasons, as McDowell and Sellars would wish to say. We may think of the information available for extraction as a manifold distributed throughout the brain – the extraction of the information is the act of the subject that unifies the manifold. This unification of the manifold brain activity is the crucial step that takes us from the physical to the mental. From the one side, the move is an act of the unifying subject; from the other side, the move is a causal process, insofar as the information extracted is the information transmitted to the brain. The information distributed throughout the brain determines the information combined in the experience.

This account gives us a way of moving on from the classical dualism of Descartes. The essence of the Cartesian dualism of matter and mind is that it is the dualism of the divisible and the indivisible. The central problem is to explain the connection of the two components. If we reconceptualize the components as the manifold and the cognitive subject, we can explain their connection through a process by which information distributed throughout an antecedent manifold is combined in the experiencing subject responsible for its extraction. This deals, indeed, with only one side of the problem, explaining how matter affects mind. I have at present no solution to the other side, no explanation of how the agent can affect the future of the world – but half a loaf is better than no bread!

3 THE PURPOSE OF SENSE EXPERIENCE

In the earlier discussion of the extraction of information, I built in the act of the subject that refers the information to its source. I was able to do this, because I was connecting the extraction of information with the act of judgment, which necessarily involves a reference to a domain that determines its truth or falsity. Sense experience, as understood so far, does not seem to involve this essential reference to a reality beyond itself. Nevertheless, it is possible to argue that sense experience also leads beyond itself, on the basis of my position that sense experience is constructed through the act of the subject in response to the incoming stimuli.

It is worth noting that the response of the organism, which is the construction of sense experience, is not the only kind of response that the creature can make to the sensory input. Sense experience, as we enjoy it, is a special *kind* of response. The familiar visual experience of human beings is associated with a functioning visual cortex. When the visual cortex is damaged, the visual experience disappears. This does not mean, however, that *all* appropriate response to visual stimuli will disappear. Human beings are also equipped with more primitive but faster working visual systems, which operate when I move my head to dodge a rock thrown towards it, although I do not actually see it coming.[7]

An interesting response to visual stimuli available to the chameleon and the cuttlefish and certain other creatures is the capacity to change the colour of the skin to match the colour of the environment. This "mechanism" operates through the optical system and parallels in a strange way our capacity to modify the visual cortex in accordance with the different wave lengths of light impinging on the retina. The purpose of the chameleon and the cuttlefish is to construct a camouflage that will foil predators. Living organisms cannot survive and have not survived without the capacity to make appropriate responses to their sensory input. A creature that has not learned to take the appropriate evasive action when pursued by a predator will not live to tell the tale.

The purpose of the chameleon in changing the colour of its skin is clear enough, but what is the purpose of sense experience? If we are prepared to describe what takes place in the construction of sense experience as an act, then this act must have a purpose. What could the purpose be? Presumably, like the camouflage of the chameleon, the general purpose is to foster the adaptation of the organism to its environment, but what is the specific purpose? My suggestion is that the purpose of the act is to represent reality. This is where the concept of representation, which is so central to the traditional theory of perception, enters the story. It is not the concept of an item that happens to appear in experience and happens to resemble some external object. Representations are deliberately constructed through an act of the subject and their purpose is to form a map of the environment that will guide the subject in achieving other purposes.

If this is correct, then it will be a complete mistake to suppose that the function of the subject is merely to contemplate a procession of sense-data in what Daniel Dennett calls the "Cartesian theatre."[8] The so-called sense-data are not really data at all: they are constructed by the subject in response to the sensory input. If the content of sense experience was merely given as a datum rather than constructed for a purpose, there would be no way to move beyond it; but if the purpose of sense experience

7 It is these more primitive systems that are invoked to explain the phenomenon of *blindsight*, discussed in chapter 1, section 4.

8 *Consciousness Explained*, 17.

is to represent reality, then a reality that transcends sense experience must be presupposed in adopting such a purpose.[9]

Since the very nature of the act of judgment is to refer an ideal content to a reality beyond the act, it is not strictly necessary to specifically mention that our purpose in using judgments is to introduce the external reality. But if it is true that the purpose behind the construction of sense experiences is the representation of reality, this will illuminate the purpose associated with the use of judgments, and explain why judgments have the special structure that we find them to have. This will, in turn, connect judgments and sense experiences in a way that will make intelligible how sense experiences can provide a foundation for judgments.

With the interpretation of sense experience as a response to sensory stimuli whose purpose is to represent reality, we are now in a position to overcome the isolation of the concept of appearance that troubled me earlier. How the object appears to me is how the object is represented by me in response to input from the senses. Appearances have found a home as components within an act of representing reality. How the world appears to me in visual experience is the visual representation of the world that I construct through utilizing visual input. Thus, the theory of appearing is not to be contrasted with the representative theory of perception – it is to be integrated within it!

A distinction is sometimes drawn between subjective and objective appearances. Roughly, the subjective appearance is how the object appears to me in my present situation, given the present condition of my sensory apparatus. The objective appearance is how the object would appear to anyone endowed with normal senses in a specified situation. For example, without my glasses lines of print appear very blurred to *me*, because of the shortcomings of my visual system. This is a *subjective* appearance. On the other hand, a straight stick half-immersed in water appears bent to *everyone*, because of the refraction of light. This is an *objective* appearance. This distinction can be reproduced within the theory of representation. The subjective representation of the object is how I actually represent the object, taking account of any peculiarities in my make-up. The objective representation is how the thing would normally be represented by a standard subject in the specified situation.

In this chapter we have explained the nature of sense experience as the response of the subject to the incoming sensory stimuli, and we have identified the purpose of this response as the representation of reality.

9 The distinction often drawn between veridical and nonveridical sense experiences itself reveals a presupposition that these experiences must be considered as representations of reality. This topic will be considered at greater length in chapter 14, section 3.

We are now faced with the problem of explaining the nature of this representation and the presupposition of reality it involves. To adopt as one's purpose the representation of reality, one must have already some conception of the reality to be represented. This conception must be a priori, since it is a condition of the possibility of every special and empirical representation of reality and hence cannot be derived from experience. We might imagine a bare consciousness of the manifold of sensory items without the involvement of conceptual activity. But for the sensory items to fulfil their function as representations of reality, a conception of the reality to be represented is necessarily presupposed. I shall leave aside until chapter 11 the detailed discussion of this a priori concept of reality. In the next chapter, I shall tackle the question of how we can form representations that correspond to reality and provide us with a reliable guide.

10

The Representation of Reality

1 SENSORY REPRESENTATIONS AND MAPS

The representation of reality is, of course, only one among the many projects of the subject or agent, and its fundamental purpose is to help us achieve our other goals. For example, one important objective is the acquisition of food, and the visual representation of the environment helps us to locate and lay hold of sources of food. That is, our visual experience will map out our route to the food source. To do this successfully, it is not necessary and not even convenient for our visual representation to be a *replication* of the actual state of affairs, even if this were possible. A map of the zoo is useful, precisely because it differs from the zoo itself in important ways. Nevertheless, the map must bear some relation to the actual zoo or it could not be considered a map of the zoo; there are also standards that the map must meet in order to be considered a good map of the zoo. A map that successfully fulfils the purpose for which it has been created will guide the visitors to the places they want to go, such as the food concession.

The sensory representations constructed by the subject in response to the sensory input are also constructed with the purpose of providing a guide to action, and they are also more or less successful in achieving this objective. The fundamental distinction in this area is not between right and wrong, but between good and bad, or perhaps between better and worse. What causes most trouble is not downright misrepresentation, but representations that are just not good enough for our purposes. For example, the main problem with visual experience is not the occasional spectacular illusion, it is poor vision. Our visual representation may not be clear enough or detailed enough to give us the information we want. Sometimes, the problem may lie in the external conditions of observation, as when we cannot make out clearly enough the road ahead because of the fog. Sometimes, the representation is blurred or clouded because the observer needs new glasses. And sometimes the representation is inadequate because of the natural limits of our visual system, as when we fail to see the micro-organisms swimming about in the water we are intending to drink.

The different ways in which our sensory representations can be unsatisfactory may be compared with the different kinds of problems we find in our maps. Some maps are poor maps, because they contain actual errors (the soviet authorities apparently used to introduce deliberate errors into the official maps of Moscow to confuse the CIA!). But we may consider a map poor if it is not sufficiently detailed for our purposes, even if it does not contain actual mistakes. A road map is a poor map if it does not mark all the minor roads, and induces us to take a wrong turn.

The comparison between visual representations and maps is a great improvement on the comparison with pictures that was often used in the past. A picture of an elephant is certainly a representation of an elephant, but although the picture and the elephant are very different in many respects – for instance, one is much heavier than the other – the picture is a good picture of the elephant only if it looks like the elephant as observed from a particular point of view. But it does not make sense to say that the sensations look like the things that produced them, since visual sensations *are* the ways things look. Thus, it does not make sense to say that visual representations are *pictures* of an external reality.

Changing the model from picturing to mapping reality de-emphasizes the role of similarity between reality and representation. This fits in very well with the change that took place during the seventeenth century, which we discussed in chapter 3. Those who championed the new science, such as Galileo, Descartes, Hobbes, Locke, and Sir Robert Boyle, wished to conceive the natural world in accordance with the categories of geometry and physics. It therefore became imperative to remove certain qualities, such as colours, from the physical world and find a new home for them in the mind. Colours were features of our sense-experiences, but there was nothing in the physical world resembling the colours we experienced.[1]

If we return to the map analogy, it was the custom at one time to colour red all areas belonging to the British Empire, while using other

---

1 As explained in chapter 3, Locke did, of course, assign to things colours as *secondary qualities*, which were nothing but powers to produce in us the colours we directly experienced.

colours for the French Empire and the Russian Empire. But even though no one supposes that the colours chosen have anything to do with the real character of these parts of the world, it can hardly be called a case of misrepresentation. Misrepresentation, on this system, would be to colour red the United States of America because it would deny the actual outcome of the American Revolution. Similarly, since the colours we experience are systematically correlated with the pigmentation of the surfaces of the things in the environment, they can be used to identify particular kinds of objects, even though these objects do not actually have the colours we experience painted on their surfaces. The experience of colours, therefore, is no hallucination. We have a hallucination, if we experience colours when nothing is there associated with and causally responsible for the colours we enjoy.[2]

2 THE PROBLEM WITH THE MAP ANALOGY

The map analogy is a definite improvement on the picture analogy, because it downplays similarity in appearance and introduces the function of the map, which is to guide behaviour. A road map shows which road to take to get to Chicago; in the same way, a visual representation may show which path to take to get to the village. Nevertheless, there remains one crucial difference between a map representation and a sensory representation. In the case of a map, we have access to both the map of the zoo and the zoo it maps, whereas in the case of sense experience we are restricted to the representation and have no access to the thing in itself. We can check the accuracy of the zoo map by observing the zoo itself, but we have no comparable way of checking the accuracy of sensory representations. Moreover, we can explain the original construction of the map of the zoo in terms of the observations of a surveyor who is able to inspect the real zoo.

This is a familiar and formidable objection. Can we retain a concept of sensory representation, given that it is impossible, even in principle, to inspect the object of representation? What remains of the concept of representation, once access to the thing represented is denied? With sensory representation, we can, indeed, retain the numerical difference between the representation and what it represents. This is possible, if we are prepared to follow the line developed in the preceding chapter

2 For a more detailed account, see the discussion of the question of colour in chapter 3, section 4.

and build into the very function of constructing representations, in response to the sensory input, an a priori conception of the object of representation. The representation is one thing and the object is another thing, just as the map is one thing and the zoo is another.

Since sensory representations – like maps – have as a central function the guiding of behaviour, just as maps may vary in quality so also sensory representations may be classified as better or worse. Since the main function of sense experience is to guide our future behaviour, we may discover that the guidance provided will be less than satisfactory, if it leads us to disaster. The disaster may be attributed to an unsatisfactory representation, just as other disasters may be blamed on inaccurate maps. In the case of a map, it is possible in principle to check its accuracy *before* disaster strikes, e.g. by hiring a helicopter to survey from above the terrain represented in the map. But there is no such way to check the accuracy of our sensory representations by comparing them with the real things.

How important is it to be able to check up on the sensory representations that we construct? We usually proceed without running a test on our sensory representations, and often we would have no time to run such a test even if it were available. Driving along a bumpy road, my visual representation of the potholes stretched out before me guides my attempts to avoid them. If through some curious illusion the position of a pothole is misrepresented, I have no time to correct the illusion before the car hits the bump. Where we have the luxury of time, a test would certainly be useful, although an infallible test is perhaps too much to hope for. But my theoretical question is whether a creature could run a system of sensory representation without any procedure for checking these representations. I see no reason to doubt this possibility. Perhaps the rabbit reacts on the basis of its visual representations, although it has no way of assessing whether the apparent fox is real or illusionary.

Although this may be true of the rabbit, the question is academic in our own case, since we certainly do have ways of checking that our experiential representations are veridical and high quality. One of the obvious facts about visual experience is that it is difficult to make out, in detail, objects that are at some distance from the observer. I may believe that I see my friend coming towards me along the road, but when he gets closer, I realize that the person coming is not my friend after all. The original visual representation was not sufficiently clear for a positive identification and I was led into error. The improved quality when the person gets closer allows me to correct my mistake.

This is a case where I change my mind about the person coming towards me on the basis of subsequent experience. Common sense would certainly endorse this change of mind, but if all we have to go on are representations, what right do we have to say that one representation is better than another? Is it simply a matter of reviewing our entire pack of representations and dismissing those that do not cohere with the main body? The majority rules, and dissidents are ignored.

This is the result we get if we construe visual experience as enjoying a series of pretty pictures that we have to divide into the sheep and the goats on the basis of some notion of coherence. Visual representations, however, are constructed with the explicit purpose of representing reality, and there are standard techniques to follow if the original representation proves unsatisfactory. For example, if I cannot make out the identity of a man in the distance, I do not have to wait for the man to come closer. I can walk towards *him* and in this way get an improved representation. I can also obtain the better quality representation by using a telescope. We also on occasion use microscopes to obtain detailed representations impossible with the naked eye. In other words, vision does not consist of a set of isolated snapshots that come out of the blue. There is looking as well as seeing, and when we look at something, we generate a series of related representations that can be checked against one another. We have ways to improve the quality when the original representations fail to satisfy us.

We are still lacking the acid test – the check against reality. In other cases, we can compare our representations against what is represented, at least in principle. Suppose I represent the sheep now in a pen by making a notch on a tally stick as each sheep passes in through the gate. I can always validate this representation by comparing the notches on the tally stick with the sheep in the pen that they represent. But there is no way to check sense experiences against the reality that transcends them.

This argument can be seen as an oversimplification, once we recognize that sense experiences should not be treated as a homogeneous class. There are various kinds of sense experiences. The usual classification is sight, hearing, smell, taste, and touch. This seems to me fair enough, provided that the sense of touch is bolstered by the kinesthetic sense, which provides information about the position of various parts of the body, including hands that are touching other objects.[3]

---

3 This rough-and-ready classification is good enough for my purposes, even though it would hardly satisfy those who seek precision in this area.

Given this variety, would it not be possible to treat sense experiences in one category as representing objects revealed through another sensory modality? For example, the characteristic smell given off by an object of a certain kind could be used to represent and identify objects of that kind. This system of representation using the sense of smell can be checked through observation of the smelly things, in the same way as the system of notches in a stick can be checked by counting the sheep in the pen.

In much the same way different foods can be represented and discriminated through the way they taste. The general validity of this system of discrimination is confirmed, for instance, by a degree of correlation with the way things look. In those cases where things that look the same taste different, we have the good sense to realize that this is because the sense of taste has uncovered differences not apparent to the naked eye.

Although we can often recognize kinds of things through the way they taste, through the smells they give off, or through the characteristic sounds they make,[4] the dominant representations of the world for human beings are those obtained through sight and touch.[5] There is some temptation to take as more fundamental the sense of touch, with its ability to locate palpable objects co-ordinated through the kinesthetic sense. Touch is certainly more primitive than vision, but in truth they are so closely integrated in our representation of the world that they are hard to separate. Hand-eye co-ordination is central to our way of operating.

One powerful argument, however, against including sight in the foundation is that there are people, blind from birth, who have to manage without it. This suggests that the sense of sight operates as an early warning system. I realize that the brick wall I see before me will block my progress when I come up against it. Other smaller objects that I see can be pushed aside and manipulated.

There are many interesting questions in this area, but I shall not pursue them any further. The fact is that however we may structure or co-ordinate the contributions of our various senses, we are never in a position to compare our sensory representations with the things themselves, with the objects that we try to depict.

---

4 Experts can identify the species of an unseen bird in the forest through its special call.

5 For bats, of course, the sense of hearing is much more important and dogs can discriminate particular individuals through their sense of smell.

3 PRIMARY AND SECONDARY REPRESENTATIONS

One way to dress up this recognition is to draw a distinction between primary representations and secondary representations.[6] Primary representations are formed by the subject in response to the sensory input; secondary representations presuppose a cognition of the object of representation, and are constructed to utilize – in a convenient package – information presented through this cognition. For example, the mapmaker employs a variety of observations of the terrain that the map depicts, and can check the accuracy of the map by further observations. In secondary representation, it is always possible in principle to check accuracy by appealing to the original cognition of the object of representation. In primary representation, there is no such appeal, since there is no cognition of the object except through the representation.

I have argued that the main function of sensory representations is to guide our actions, and that these representations can be evaluated as more or less successful in carrying out this function. So how can our sense experiences be as successful as they usually are in guiding action, unless they correspond in some way to the stage upon which we are called to perform? And it is natural to explain at least some of our failures by claiming that our sense experience does not correspond in the usual way to what is really there. But what is the precise nature of this correspondence (or lack of correspondence) between representation and reality?

In the case of secondary representation, we are always able to specify the nature and criteria of this correspondence with the object. Suppose a medieval duke attempts to represent the weapons possessed by a neighbouring baron by laying out on the floor of his own armoury the appropriate number of swords, battle axes, etc. The nature of the correspondence and the criteria for correct representation are both perfectly clear. In the case of a map, the criteria of correspondence are also clear, once the scale and projection have been specified.[7] But although we can and must say that there is a correspondence between our sense

---

6 An alternative terminology would be to use "presentation" for what I have called "primary representation" and "representation" *tout court* in place of my "secondary representation." Although this alternative has some merit, I decided against it because it downplays the analogy between the two forms of representation. Moreover, even a primary representation is a re-enactment of the information contained in its antecedents.

7 The criteria for the correct use of a representational system are in fact incredibly varied, especially when there is a use of symbols whose function is established by convention.

experience and the reality beyond, we cannot explain the specific nature of the correspondence. Any attempt to do so must bring in inappropriate models drawn from other schemes of correspondence, where
we do understand how the system works. The kind of correspondence
operating in the case of primary representation cannot be elucidated
through notions drawn from any scheme of secondary representation.
We have seen why the tempting idea that sensory representations are
mental pictures of the world must break down. We now see that even
the superior "map" analogy cannot help us. But this does not prevent us
from affirming some form of correspondence between sensory representation and reality, using a *general* notion abstracted from the various
special cases of correspondence with which we are familiar.

This appeal to a generic notion can frustrate the objection that the
idea of a correspondence between sense experience and reality is incoherent, but it is merely a defensive move that is not very illuminating. We
have merely provided a logical space for some form of correspondence
between sense experience and reality without any explanation of how
this could come about. But the situation is transformed if we are allowed
to bring in our central doctrine that sense experience is a response to
the sensory input. The sense experience can be said to correspond to the
sensory input, because it varies with the sensory input. The experience
would have been different if the input had been different.

That is to say, the correspondence between sense experience and sensory input is like the correspondence between effects and causes. An
effect is not required to resemble its cause, although it may do so. What
is required is that effects vary with causes, so that similar causes have
similar effects. By and large, similar effects are also produced by similar
causes, although we allow a little latitude to take care of the possibility
that the same effect may be produced in different ways through different sets of antecedent causes.

The parallels between the kind of correspondence involved in the
causal relation and in sensory representation are no accident. The traditional theory interpreted sense experiences as sensations – as effects generated by antecedent causes. In replacing this theory with the doctrine
that sense experience is a response to a stimulus, we are not denying a
causal relation between sense experience and its antecedents, but rather
re-interpreting this within a richer conceptual scheme. The idea of a response assigns to the consequent rather than the antecedent the activity
constituting the relation.[8]

8 See the detailed discussion in chapter 9, section 2.

It is important to be clear that sensations are to be regarded as representations not because we have *recognized* a causal relation between these sensations and their antecedents, but rather because of the *existence* of a causal relation between the representations and the antecedents to which we respond. If we could not construct representations until we were aware of a causal relation between the inner items and the external world, the situation would be hopeless, since there is no awareness of an external world except through the construction of representations. The *recognition* of a causal relation between sense experience and its antecedents occurs only at a later point in the development of our system of knowledge, once the cognition of an objective domain of things and events has been established through our sensory representations.[9]

---

[9] This is, of course, the point made in chapter 2, in which the traditional theory comes back to life.

11

The Presupposition of Reality

1 THE SCEPTICAL OBJECTION

In the previous chapter, I tried to explain how it is possible to represent a reality to which access is denied. This explanation will be successful only if one concedes the legitimacy of the presupposition of reality built into the response of the subject. I shall begin by facing an objection from the side of the sceptic. Even if it is true that anyone whose purpose is the representation of reality must have some a priori conception of reality and must believe in a reality transcending experience, how can we be sure that this belief is correct? After all, anyone whose purpose is to reach El Dorado must believe in the existence of El Dorado, but this does not preclude its being a mere figment of the imagination. Is it not logically possible that the universal belief in a reality that transcends our representations is also a delusion?

The a priori concept of reality and the empirical concept of El Dorado are, however, very different in nature, and it is a mistake to argue that what applies to empirical concepts may also apply in the other case. There is nothing corresponding to the empirical concept of a city whose streets are paved with gold, but it does not follow that there may be nothing corresponding to the a priori concept of reality. Indeed, in denying that the name "El Dorado" denotes a real object, we are presupposing a domain of reality where nothing that answers to the description of El Dorado is to be found. This means that in order to deny that there is anything corresponding to a given concept, we must presuppose something that corresponds to the concept of reality.

2 KANT AND BRADLEY

The theory I am proposing has a certain Kantian ring to it, and it looks as if my a priori conception of reality may be closely related to Kant's a priori concept of the object in general, which for Kant defines the essence of the understanding. Cognition, for Kant, is essentially the cognition of objects and is governed by a general concept instantiated by any and every object. Although it is tempting to suppose that the concept of reality and the concept of the object in general may be different versions of the same idea, there is, in fact, an important difference between them. The conception of reality is fundamental and the concept of the object in general is a more special function necessary for the representation of objects within reality. To represent a defined object of any kind as an object, the concept of the object in general must be presupposed. Kant argued, indeed, that the object in general was further determined through a system of twelve pure concepts of the understanding, associated with the formal logic of his day, but I shall not take time to discuss this elaboration. The fundamental point I want to make is that the conception of reality is just not the concept of an object at all.

The position developed here is closer to the objective idealism sponsored at the end of the nineteenth century by F.H. Bradley and others. In his *Principles of Logic*, Bradley defines the act of judgment as "the act which refers an ideal content ... to a reality beyond the act."[1] We might very well think that all this means is that in one judgment we refer the colour blue to the sofa and in another judgment we refer the colour red to the carpet, so that different judgments may be about different realities or real things. But this is what Bradley cannot allow. He argues that in the last analysis a plurality of reals is impossible. To conceive a plurality of reals is to conceive *a* plurality or *one* plurality. The conception is impossible without the combination of the manifold into a single aggregate that is Reality. The specific judgments introduced above must now be rephrased. "The sofa is blue" becomes "Reality is such that the sofa is blue": and "The carpet is red" becomes "Reality is such that the carpet is red."

Bradley's argument for this uncompromising Monism may be somewhat dubious, because it rules out the possibility of a plural reference to a number of real things without combining these things into one big thing, or even one set to which they are all supposed to belong.[2] Nevertheless, his conception of a single, all-embracing, undifferentiated reality seems very close to what I am saying we must presuppose a priori if we are to adopt the purpose of constructing representations. Bradley's description of the ultimate reality in fact goes well beyond the idea I have built into the function of representation. In his metaphysical treatise *Appearance and Reality* we find: "The Absolute is one system ... a single

---

1 *Principles of Logic*, second edition, 10.
2 For a careful discussion of plural reference, see Laycock, *Words without Objects*, chapter 2.

and all-embracing experience, which embraces every partial diversity in concord" (146–7). For Bradley the absolute reality presupposed in the act of judgment is experience. The Absolute must be experience, because nothing else can be considered real. "Sentient experience, in short, is reality, and what is not this is not real" (145). The only way to give a meaning to this fundamental notion of experience is through an appeal to the experience each person enjoys. Not that the immediate experience enjoyed by each finite centre is to be identified with the Absolute. The road from my immediate experience to the system of experience that is the Absolute leads through the distinctions and abstractions of thought, and is difficult and treacherous; I do not propose to follow along the path mapped out in Bradley's dialectic. My concern is with the notion of experience with which he begins. Since the notion of experience is not the concept of an object, Bradley's view that reality is experience suggests an alternative to the natural idea that the conception of reality is the concept of a kind of object, although Bradley himself never used, or even seemed to notice, the crucial distinction.

We may, however, accept the suggestion that the reality presupposed in the cognitive response to the sensory input is not to be conceived as some kind of object without having to subscribe to the view that reality is experience. Bradley himself certainly identifies reality and experience, but it is possible to develop a version of his essential theory that makes no such identification. C.A. Campbell has proposed a variant of Bradley's theory in which he adopts a more sceptical stance, and backs away from the claim that the absolute reality presupposed in the act of judgment must be conceived as experience. In *Scepticism and Construction* Campbell writes: "It may very well be that while everything which finite mind, with its deficient equipment, can regard as 'fact' is charged with the character of 'experience,' *the* fact, genuine Reality, is not" (47). I am much happier with Campbell's generic version, and feel no reason to suppose that reality must have the special character of experience. I wish to retain, however, the insight that the idea of reality presupposed in the construction of representations is not the concept of an object.

3 MASS TERMS

We are helped by an illuminating development in logic to make sense of an idea of reality that is not the concept of some object. In recent years there has been an important discussion of mass terms or mass nouns, which proved hard to fit into the dominant logic of *Principia Mathematica*. These are ideas like the idea of water, the idea of gold, and the idea of stuff or matter. These terms do not refer to the objects that can be comfortably substituted for the individual variables in the modern logic system. The term "water" does not refer to an object, although there are *parcels* of water that are objects, such as the water in my glass and the water in the pool on the floor, just as there are many objects *made* of gold. My suggestion is that "reality" is a mass term, like "water." Although there are *parcels* of reality that are real objects, Reality as such is not an object. We are not forced to believe that the reference to reality built into our system of representation must be a reference to some object or set of objects.

When we are using count nouns, the relevant question is "How many?" "How many horses are there in the field?" When we are using mass nouns, the question is "How much?" "How much water is there in the pail?" We could answer the question about horses by saying, perhaps: "There is a small *number* of horses in the field." The answer to the question about water might be: "There is a small *amount* of water in the pail."

The problem posed for modern logic by the widespread use of mass nouns has been addressed by W.V.O. Quine. The picture to which he seems to subscribe is that such expressions belong to an archaic or "juvenile" level that has been superseded by an "adult" dichotomy of "singular and general" terms – a dichotomy that does conform to the canonical notation of modern logic.[3] He writes in his paper "Speaking of Objects": "We persist in breaking reality down somehow into a multiplicity of identifiable and discriminable objects to be referred to by singular and general terms" (1).

The more primitive system involving mass terms does not, however, simply disappear when superseded by the mature system with its singular and general terms. It stays around to challenge the claim of the modern system of logic to be fully comprehensive. To answer this challenge, a way must be found to fit the recalcitrant mass terms into the canonical system.[4]

This is attempted by Quine himself in *Word and Object* #20. Quine asserts that in the sentence "Water is a liquid" the mass term "water" functions as a concrete singular term in much the same way as the proper name "Agnes" in the sentence "Agnes is a lamb." The only difference is that whereas the object to which Agnes refers comes in a neat package, the term "Water" designates a single "scattered" object. This is certainly

---

3 Cf. H. Laycock, *Words without Objects*, 15.

4 "While the so-called 'mass nouns' are widely perceived to resist assimilation into Quine's basic 'canonical notation,' the first-order calculus of predicates, one chief response to this is to contrive some strategy, whereby, ironically, resistance can be somehow overcome." Laycock, *Words without Objects*, 14.

ingenious, but in *Words without Objects* Henry Laycock has argued persuasively that it will not do. For one thing, it is possible to imagine another lamb qualitatively identical with but numerically distinct from Agnes, whereas "the notion of a liquid numerically distinct though qualitatively indistinguishable from water ... is just plain incoherent" (175).

Moreover, if Quine were to push his analysis, it would certainly embarrass him in the special case of the term "reality." Quine is not averse to talking about reality. For instance, he mentions reality in the quotation from "Speaking of Objects" introduced earlier in this section: "We persist in breaking *reality* down somehow into a multiplicity of identifiable and discriminable objects."[5] What is this noun "reality" that Quine is using so confidently? It is clearly a mass term, and if Quine's account of mass terms is accepted, it will refer to a single, perhaps not scattered, but at least dispersed, object. If Reality is a single thing, denoted by a singular term, we are getting very close to Bradley's Monism. The Absolute is One. We can even reinforce the comparison by taking Quine's multiplicity of discriminable objects to correspond to the "Appearances" of Bradley.

To be fair, there is an obvious countermove that Quine and his supporters might make. In the mature system, the term "reality" will drop out, to be replaced by an apparatus of quantifiers. Bradley's standard formula for the act of judgment is: "Reality is such that S is P." For the supporter of modern logic, the use of the noun "Reality" in this expression makes no sense. The formula is to be rewritten using quantifiers, e.g. "There is an x such that Sx and Px." The term "reality" is a kind of ladder, as used in Wittgenstein's *Tractatus*, to be thrown away once the new system is a going concern.

This countermove, however, is far from satisfactory. Even in the *Tractatus*, the throwing away of the ladder used to reach an understanding of the final picture is widely regarded as highly suspicious. In the case of the term "reality," the existential quantifier replacing it in the predicate calculus has a meaning, when used concretely,[6] which appears to have the notion of reality built into it.

We may conclude, then, with some confidence that the noun "reality" is a mass noun belonging to a grammatical category not easily handled in Russell's logic. It is ironic that the central concept of reality in Bradley's metaphysics cannot be handled by Russell's logical system, not because it is necessarily spurious and illegitimate, but because the logic of *Principia Mathematica* itself fails to cover all there is.

---

5 Emphasis mine.

6 The contrast is with the formal counterpart of the predicate calculus where the symbols have been drained of all meaning.

The thesis I wish to advance, then, is that the original conception of the transcendent built into our response to the sensory input is not a concept of an object but the mass concept of reality. Reality is not conceived as an object; the word is a mass term, like "water" and "stuff." To posit the mass concept of reality as the fundamental idea in our cognitive system is indeed to displace Kant's concept of the object in general from its central position. The concept of the object in general governs Quine's "multiplicity of identifiable and discriminable objects," whereas the mass concept of reality is associated with the reality that is broken down in this way.

4 THE INFRA-RATIONAL

Although I agree with both Bradley and Campbell that reality as such cannot be captured through the categories and processes of thought that introduce standard physical objects, there is an important difference in how I imagine the alternative. The idealists are thinking of reality as being somehow *above* thought – Reality is the Supra-rational! I am going the other way and imagine reality as *below* the level of thought – Reality is the Infra-rational! For Campbell in particular the infinity of reality is essentially the infinity of the divine, and the ultimate nature of reality is no more accessible to us than is the nature of God in mystical theology.[7] For me, the infinity of reality is more akin to the infinity of Aristotelian prime matter, which is, being absolutely formless, too formless for the mind to get a grip on.

The idea is that the reality presupposed by the act of judgment is introduced *below* the level of explicit thought about the various objects populating the universe. This offers real help with a puzzle that worried the later British Idealists. The standard idealist doctrine is that "in judgment the ultimate logical subject is always 'Reality.'"[8] The formula is: "Reality is such that *S* is *P*." The problem is to reconcile this global doctrine with our ordinary conception of the distinction between subject and predicate. Usually, in judgment, we have an object or event that is the subject and a predicate we use to characterize this object or event. Campbell's solution is "to distinguish between the *ultimate* and the *immediate* subject of judgment" (238). Although we may use the ideal content in the mind to isolate the immediate subject, we must regard this special subject as "that part of the presupposed independent reality which in our judging

7 See, for instance, *On Selfhood and Godhood*, chapter 16 "Otto and the Numinous: The Transition to Supra-rational Theism."
8 C.A. Campbell, *In Defence of Free Will*, 238.

activity at any particular moment we are seeking to know" (240). That is, to solve his problem, Campbell must treat the reality presupposed in judgment as having *parts*. Although the idea of a part of reality is more general than the idea of a part of a spatial reality or a part of a temporal reality, it is difficult to see what Campbell could have had at the back of his mind other than parts of space, when invoking physical objects as special subjects, or parts of time, when the special subjects are events.

5 SPACE AND TIME

Bradley would certainly regard the suggestion that reality is a spatio-temporal manifold within which we may introduce parts as a total perversion of his insight. There is a tradition running through philosophy from the time of Plato according to which the things that come to be and pass away are less real than the things that do not, such as the eternal forms. The supra-rationalist imagines a reality that is an absolute unity and does not consist of a plurality of things following one another in time. Such things are mere appearances, of uncertain status. The infra-rationalist, on the other hand, envisages a reality that is a manifold, designated by a mass term, within which we can separate distinct regions.

This leads to the idea that reality is basically a reality in space and time. Like the term "reality," "space" and "time" are also mass terms that do not designate an object. Perhaps the representation of a manifold of space and time is also built into the representation of reality, which is the a priori condition of our cognitive response to the sensory input. This may be a bit of a leap, but it is not an unreasonable one. It also brings us back closer to Kant. The understanding, whose essence is defined by the pure concept of the object in general, is not the only cognitive faculty posited by Kant. Kant also introduces the faculty of intuition, which he explicitly recognizes as a cognitive faculty (A 19 B 33). For Kant, there are the two forms of intuition, space and time. The original representations of space and time are in each case representations of an indeterminate, unlimited manifold sustaining relations of whole to part. Kant focuses on the pure intuitions of space and time, partly because he wishes to provide a manifold of pure intuition to enable the constructions of pure geometry and to serve as a foundation for synthetic a priori statements. But if we turn our attention to the concrete empirical intuition – involving sensations – that is conditioned by these forms, we may find underlying the various empirical intuitions something coming close to an a priori idea of reality. Kant himself does not explore whether other a priori factors may be necessary for empirical *intuition* over and above the forms of space and time, although he does refer to "the real that is an object of sensation," (B 207) which is at least close to the mass notion of reality.[9]

We may want to say that the faculty of sensibility is the source of *mass* nouns, and the understanding, with its governing concept of the object in general, is the source of *count* nouns. This would allow me to give due recognition to the fact that the relation between Reality and realities, Space and spaces, Time and times is not the relation of universal to instances but the relation of whole to parts. It allows me to introduce a priori the domain of particularity that must be presupposed if we are to be able to posit, through the function of the understanding, the individual objects that are the particular instances of general concepts. Thus, if we can associate our a priori representation of reality built into our response to the sensory input with our a priori representations of space and time, we can get a better grip on what it means to treat "reality" as a mass noun. If the real is what occupies space, then just as we can have an amount of space, there is also an amount of reality occupying that space.

This association of *reality* with space and time, however, conflicts dramatically with Kant's central theory of the transcendental *ideality* of space and time. Kant's contention that the pure intuitions of space and time have their "seat in the subject only" (B 41) is surprising and disturbing. It is upsetting to be told that space and time are not ultimately real, but it would be downright paradoxical if it were suggested that even the reality presupposed in our response to sensory input is not really real.[10]

It looks very like a contradiction to suggest that what we refer to by the term "reality" may be merely ideal, but it is even difficult to give a meaning to Kant's claim that space and time are merely ideal. Kant is on firm ground when he argues that our original representations of space and time are pure intuitions of an unlimited manifold, and that these intuitions are conditions of the possibility of representing particular objects in space and particular events in time. But what could it mean to claim that what is intuited is not real? Kant objects to admitting that there are "two eternal and infinite self-subsistent non-entities (space and time), which are there (yet without there being anything real) only in order to

---

9 The situation is complicated because Kant introduces the *categories* of reality, negation and limitation in the *Anticipations of Perception* (A 166-176 B 207-218). I would want to distinguish the original representation of reality from the *category* of reality, in much the same way as Kant himself distinguishes the original unity of apperception from the *category* of unity (B 131).

10 Kant does indeed introduce a notion of *empirical reality* which is compatible with *transcendental ideality*. This permits us to continue using empirical discourse in the usual way, ignoring the revelations of critical philosophy.

contain in themselves all that is real" (A 39 B 56). The answer is to argue that space and time are not real objects, not because they are not real, but because they are not objects. Kant contends that a real time "would be something which would be actual and yet not an actual object" (A 32 B 49). This is no paradox, but the sober truth, once we recognize that the terms "space" and "time" are mass terms referring to manifolds.

It is of vital importance to challenge Kant's position that the pure intuitions of space and time are rooted exclusively in the cognitive subject, since, if he is right, there is no way in which different people could communicate about the same real world. If we are to communicate, your time will be my time and your space, my space. Moreover, if we accept the reality of space and time, it is much easier to make sense of Kant's theory that the objects of our empirical knowledge are transcendentally ideal, due to the fact that such objects depend on the combination of the manifold through an act of the understanding. It is difficult to grasp how objects of cognition can require the subject to combine a given manifold without these objects becoming dependent on the subject in an unhealthy way (it is not healthy for these objects to be inaccessible to other cognitive subjects).

There is a model that may help[11] if we are prepared to allow that sets have no standing apart from the combination of the elements they contain through the act of the subject by which the set is formed. Nevertheless, because we assume the objective reality of the elements the set contains, we cannot reduce this set to a mere idea in the mind. The set of horses in the field does not exist in my mind. Moreover, if your set contains the same elements as my set, according to the axiom of extensionality from orthodox set theory, they will be the very same set. Different people will be able to talk about the same set. In the same way, we may argue that our familiar physical objects cannot be posited except through an act of the understanding by which the manifold that they contain is combined in one object. Such objects will be transcendentally ideal, since they have no being apart from the synthesis of the understanding. Nevertheless, your objects may be the same as my objects if they contain the same manifold. We can refer to the same things if we carve up the manifold reality in the same way.

We can avail ourselves of this model, however, only if the manifold reality you combine is the same as the reality I combine. The manifold of pure intuition, space and time, at the very least must be the same for

---

11 For a more detailed explanation of this point, see my paper "The Transcendental Ideality of Sets and Objects."

you as it is for me. Because the manifold of empirical intuition,[12] according to Kant, corresponds to sensation, which may differ from person to person, we can live with a certain variation in the empirical manifold, even if this may lead to variations in the objects we construct and disagreements about what is really there. There may, indeed, be differences in the objects we construct without a difference in the manifold of empirical intuition, if our different histories have supplied us with a different repertoire of empirical concepts to control the combinations. This makes good sense, because we know that there are disagreements among people about what is out there, although not so serious that they cause our common world to fall apart. We disagree where we are expecting agreement.

6 THE FUTURE

I have now moved from the austere position that the cognitive response to the sensory input involves a presupposition of reality to the more specific thesis that the reality presupposed is a reality in space and time. It is hard to deny that the world as we know it is in space and time, but is there any reason to believe that it must be represented in this way? For Kant, the necessity comes from the (quasi-contingent) fact that space and time happen to be the forms of *our* intuition. He does not have an argument to show that the forms of intuition associated with any understanding must be those forms that we happen to have.[13]

There is, however, one powerful argument to integrate *time*, at any rate, as necessary for the representation of reality. This was not available to Kant in the *Critique of Pure Reason*, because of his strategy in that book of separating the theoretical and the practical. In the theory I have been elaborating, the representation of reality, which is sense experience, has as its purpose the guiding of action. A plan of action of any complexity involves the representation of a goal or objective and the representation of a means to that objective. Not only are the achievement of the goal and the carrying out of the means imagined in the future, but they are imagined at different times in the future. We think of ourselves as carrying out the means *first*, and achieving the goal *second*. Once we get the

12 The discussion is, of course, restricted to *outer* intuition, which introduces the problem of the common, objective world. I do not share with other people the experiences given through inner sense, even if we may share the same future!

13 He does say, indeed: "This mode of intuiting in space and time need not be limited to human sensibility. It may be that all finite thinking beings necessarily agree with man in this respect, although we are not in a position to judge whether this is actually so" (B 72).

idea that among future things some are more future than others, we can always imagine after the achievement of some goal events that take place even later (which we may call "the consequences"). Also, given two future events one of which is more remote than the other, we can always in principle imagine a third event that is later than the one and earlier than the other. In this way, the future can be constructed as an infinite extensive continuum.[14]

Thus, the reality we represent is the future reality, which is necessarily distinct from its representation, because the representation is *now*, whereas the reality imagined in the future is *not yet*. Although we have got used to assuming a cognitive relation between the act of knowledge and the object of knowledge, between our thinking about something and what we think about, the nature of the connection between knowledge and its object is a bit of a mystery, gnawing at the back of the mind. The cognitive relation is so very different from the other physical relations we are familiar with that it is difficult to understand how the representation in the subject can be distinct from the object represented, and yet connected to it. Perhaps we can illuminate the mystery of cognition by bringing in another mystery – the mystery of the future. Our capacity to predict in some degree future events seems particularly baffling, since the future events we think about do not exist, not yet! But perhaps it is this very case that will lead us to understand the essence of cognition. In this case cognition is not a relation between things that co-exist, but neither is it merely a relation between what exists – the prediction – and what does not. If the prediction is successful, what will be will be. The cognitive relation will hold between what is (the prediction) and what will be (the event predicted). Only if the prediction fails will the predicted event not take place, but then we have neither knowledge nor a cognitive relation.

In suggesting that it is our knowledge of the future that is fundamental and most illuminating, I do not wish to deny, of course, that we can have knowledge of the present and the past. The future is represented as the future from the point of view of the present, but in imagining a future state of myself, I realize that from the point of view of that future state, my present state will be in the past. Once I have the notion of my present state as in the past of my future state, I can introduce a more remote past for my future state that will be in the past of my present state. In this way

14 This assumes that the two events have been reduced in duration so that they are neither overlapping nor contiguous. There are, of course, practical difficulties in the way of carrying this process very far and theoretical difficulties in the way of imagining the constitution of the extensive continuum through its completion.

I will have within my ken the entire temporal continuum of past, present, and future. Although my present state is very special as the foundation of my subjective point of view, the future state posited in the construction of the continuum of time is neither special nor unique. Any point in my future can be used without changing the temporal continuum introduced. When I get up in the morning, I can think of my present state as in the past of my breakfast, my lunch, and my dinner, all of which are still to come. In this way the temporal continuum has no special origin through which it is defined, and even my present state appears within it as an ordinary citizen. We have constructed the temporal branch of what Thomas Nagel has called "The View from Nowhere." Once we have available the entire canvas of time, it is possible on the basis of evidence derived from causal regularities to posit events that took place in the past as easily as events that will take place in the future.

What about space? It may be that I introduce space into my cognition, because I am not just an agent, but also a locomotive. To man the spectator and man the agent we must add man the locomotive! It is not just that I make various plans about the future from amongst which I have to choose; I also envisage myself as moving about in the future. Movement presupposes not just time, but also change of place. To represent myself as moving about, I must introduce a system of places within which I can change. Perhaps we represent the spatial by imagining motion through space, abstracting from the direction of the locomotion from A to B in order to introduce the distance between A and B.[15] If I can assume regular processes, I can measure the distance covered and the time it takes. With a thousand paces, the Roman soldier could measure out a mile. The time this takes could also be a measure of time, although we find it more convenient to rely on the regular motions of the heavenly bodies.

So long as one is prepared to agree that the indeterminate representation of reality built into the cognitive response to the sensory input is somehow structured to involve the representation of an unlimited and ordered manifold of space and time, it is not necessary to accept my story about how this representation, which founds our conception of an objective world, came into being. I have made what I hope is a plausible attempt to link the a priori presuppositions of our cognitive capacity to our nature as movers and doers, but we are dealing here with matters that are deeply veiled, and I make no claim that I can enforce my solution.

15 Kant appears to endorse this view. "To know anything in space (for instance, a line), I must draw it" (B 137-8).

12

The Detailed Knowledge of the World

1 IDEAL CONTENT

If the a priori representation of reality is the representation of a spatio-temporal reality, then we do have an element of structure built into what is represented, which will make possible a detailed account of a system of objects. But the purely formal concept of reality built into our response to the sensory input leaves completely indeterminate the reality that is the object of cognition. Even if supplemented by the structures provided by space and time, our representation of reality remains completely formal. So how do we acquire a detailed knowledge of the reality that we originally conceive in these general terms? The a priori representation of space provides us with different places in which things may exist, and the a priori representation of time provides us with different times at which events may occur. We know a priori that these various places are all parts of a single all-embracing space, but how do we know what exists in these places? We know a priori that these various times are all parts of a single all-embracing time, but how do we know what takes place at these times?

To simplify the argument, for the time being I shall restrict my account to the case of space. The bare minimum we can know if we are to have empirical knowledge at all is that what exists in one place is similar to (or different from) what exists in another place. An amazing system of different places has been organized in accordance with Euclidean geometry (with further refinements for the purposes of modern physics), but we do not have to suppose that cognitive subjects necessarily began with anything this sophisticated.

Even if we do not require an insight into the true essence of the object, but merely a knowledge of similarities and differences, how can even this much be achieved? There is only one possible answer. Our detailed knowledge of the similarities and differences of the things in space must have something to do with the input coming from the environment through the senses into the cognitive system. It is this input that provides the necessary information.

Sense experience, as I have argued, is the response of the cognitive subject, which extracts the information available in the sensory input. But how can we move from this sense experience, produced in us by external causes, to bring into being a determinate knowledge of the reality that produced it? The distinction I drew between the transmission and the extraction of information in chapter 8, section 4 certainly does help. If sense experience is merely the reception of information transmitted from associated physiological processes in the brain, then what is happening is merely that the information is passed further down the line, in the way in which Hume conceives the derivation of ideas from impressions. But if sense experience involves a special function I call the *extraction* of information, then not only is the manifold of information distributed throughout the underlying physiological processes *combined* in the experience, but also a reference is introduced to what the information informs about. Thus, the extraction of information about an object constitutes the representation of that object.

At the time I originally introduced the notion of the extraction of information, I was in no position to explain how this was possible. Now that I understand the extraction of information as the way in which the subject responds to the incoming stimuli, I have been able to argue that the purpose controlling this kind of response involves a presupposition of a reality to be represented through the act of the subject. This provides us with a place to put the objects about which we think we have been informed, especially if the reality we imagine is a manifold of space and time.

What is still not settled, however, is the nature of the representations through which we discriminate the objects we take to populate our world. If we attack the question at the highest level and focus on that explicit knowledge of the world that can be expressed in language and involves propositions, it is clear that such a knowledge of a determinate reality necessarily involves the use of general concepts, as indeed does the planning of behaviour facilitated by this knowledge of reality. The judgment "It is night" uses a concept that also applied to the night before.[1] The judgment is based on a particular experience of darkness

---

1 This is a simpler judgment if we imagine it made by primitive man, who does not realise that it may be night here and day somewhere else.

enjoyed by the judging subject. How do we get from this particular experience to an objective knowledge of the condition of the world?

We can get help, perhaps, from a distinction drawn by F.H. Bradley. For Bradley, the appearance present in immediate experience necessarily has two sides to it. "There is a 'what' and a 'that,' an existence and a content, and the two are inseparable."[2] For Bradley, however, the essence of thought is just the separation of content from existence. Because of this separation or abstraction of an ideal content, thought is very different from reality, which demands the integration of content and existence. Thus, the logical ideas or ideal contents or concepts used in thinking are very different from the psychological ideas or impressions and images that form the mainstay of the empiricist theory of the association of ideas. Hume's impressions and ideas were considered complete and distinct existences, but as Bradley argued,[3] it was not possible to understand cognition in these terms.[4]

The power of thought is to separate the ideal content from its concrete setting and refer it elsewhere in an act of judgment, provided that there is an elsewhere to which to refer it.[5] What is elsewhere is what conforms to the ideal content or logical idea – there is no way in which the psychological idea can be moved out of the mind. One complication is that there are varying levels of abstraction and various levels of generality in the concepts we employ. How do we decide on the level of generality at which we set the ideal that we refer to reality? The animal before me may be conceptualized as a spaniel or as a dog or as an animal or in some other way. Which concept I select must depend on my special purposes. If there is a sign in the park stipulating "No Dogs," the by-law enforcement officer will classify the animal as a dog in order to justify his

---

2 *Appearance and Reality*, 162.

3 *Principles of Logic*, book 2, part 1, chapter 1 "The Theory of the Association of Ideas."

4 The parting of the ways is clearly revealed in Frege's influential paper "On Sense and Meaning." Frege distinguishes the sense of a sign from the associated idea. This idea he considers an internal image, which is merely a part or a mode of the individual mind. This is what Bradley calls the "psychological idea." Because Frege does not introduce the "logical idea" in the way Bradley does, he attaches a general content to a sign as its sense. This moves signs and particularly words to the centre of the stage in the study of thinking and constitutes the essence of the linguistic turn in contemporary philosophy. *Translations from the Philosophical Writings by Gottlob Frege*, edited by Peter Geach and Max Black, 159–60.

5 The classical sense-datum theory foundered because it could not provide access to anything other than sense-data. This defect I have remedied by introducing a suitable domain through an original mass concept of reality structured in accordance with the forms of time and space.

removal of the offending beast. A person may, of course, apply two or more concepts to the same object either successively or even at the same time, but there is no way, in practice, to apply to the object all possible concepts that might be used to categorize it. A selection must be made, depending on actual purposes.

The link between concepts and purposes can be tightened if we are prepared to stipulate that objects brought under the same concept are deemed to be equivalent for some purpose. This is obvious enough in cases where the purpose is built into the definition of the concept. Edible things fall under the concept of the edible because of their connection with the function of eating. In other cases it may be harder to show that things falling under the same concept are similar because they are equivalent for some purpose, rather than equivalent for some purpose because they are similar.

Whatever one may think about the above suggestion, my important message is that the abstraction of the ideal content from immediate experience would not take place apart from the purpose of representing and characterizing the reality beyond experience, a purpose closely associated with our other purposes and objectives. Without this purpose, we would simply enjoy the given experience in all its glory. Lacking any guidance about the level of abstraction to employ, a guidance that comes from the purposes and interests dominating our concern at the time, we would simply not abstract at all. Thus, thinking and the use of concepts does not begin with an effort to describe and classify the various sensations we enjoy. From the first, it is directed towards the cognition of an external reality. The original function of concepts is not to classify the impressions of sense but to constitute a cognition of an object that transcends these impressions.

Thought and judgment presuppose an original apprehension of an indeterminate reality, whose manifold we represent as structured in space and time. Through thought and judgment this indeterminate reality is determined. Since the original act of conception presupposed by the function of representation is the conception of reality, it makes sense that the original concepts associated with sensation will be determinations of this original concept of reality. If we are entitled to regard reality as involving a manifold of space and time, we will be able to construct objects and events that combine definite quanta of space and time. This is where we may bring in Kant's pure concept of the object in general, which I have distinguished from the original conception of reality. Specific concepts determining the things present in reality must conform to this pure concept of the object.[6] These specific concepts must somehow be associated with the various sensations produced in us by external causes, or rather, with the various sensory representations that we generate in response to the sensory input. The sensations somehow provide the stuffing for the concepts through which we discriminate the similarities and differences of the things in the external domain.

Thus, I reject the traditional story that we begin by referring the ideal content back to the experience from which it has been drawn and then make inferences to a reality that transcends this experience. I favour the alternative account that thinking does *not* begin with a description of the immediate experience that provides the platform for the act of thought. Since the whole point of separating the ideal content is to refer it elsewhere, the separating and the reference elsewhere are two faces of the same act. The abstraction of the content takes place in the context of an act of judgment that refers the content to a reality transcending the act. The purpose of such judgments is to characterize the domain in which we are called upon to act, so that we can make intelligent plans for appropriate action.

I have argued that it is the level of generality built into plans appropriate in the situation that determines the level of abstraction involved in the separation of the ideal content. This means that there can be no first step in cognition consisting in a conceptualization of given sensations, isolated from the consideration of the external domain, which is the theatre in which our purposes are enacted. In this isolation, how could we decide among the many levels of abstraction which are available?

2 NON-CONCEPTUAL CONTENT

In the previous section I have argued that the explicit knowledge of the external world constituted by acts of judgment and expressed in declarative sentences involves the abstraction of the concepts that must be employed. But should we say that sense experience as such necessarily involves conceptual content? This was an important question left undecided near the end of the section on John McDowell (chapter 8, section 3). McDowell believes that it does, on the ground that our beliefs about the world must have a justification in sense experience, and such a justification must take place within a space of reasons introducing concepts. I countered this argument by contending that a justification of

6 Kant, of course, using as his clue the structure of the formal logic of his day, worked out a complex system of twelve categories to which all possible objects of human knowledge must conform. This is not the place to try to evaluate this brilliant adventure of ideas.

empirical beliefs, properly so called, can take place only on a second pass, where we support judgments about the external world by an inference from judgments about the relevant sense experiences. This pattern of reasoning cannot be transferred, however, to explain the possibility of the judgments about sense experiences that supply the premises, nor indeed, the original knowledge of the world as a causal system presupposed in the operation of this pattern.

Although the move I have made frustrates McDowell's attempt to close out the possibility of sense experiences with non-conceptual content, it does not positively establish that there are any such experiences. We certainly do not need experiences with conceptual content to provide justifications through the use of the pattern of inference at the heart of the traditional theory of perception. So long as the sense experiences are conceived as effects with a definite character regularly produced by specific external causes, we can legitimately infer beliefs about the causes that produced them. But this is not a positive proof that there really are sense experiences that do not involve conceptual factors.

In order to argue against McDowell that the justification of our empirical beliefs through experience takes place at a high level on a second pass, I could operate with the most simplified story about how these beliefs were originally acquired. It was enough to say that we reach these beliefs on the basis of sensations produced in us by external causes. I have already argued, however, that this very simple story is just not good enough and leaves us with a huge gap between the causal and the cognitive. I have tried to close the gap by replacing the idea that sense experience is a mere effect of external causes with the theory that sense experience is an active response of the cognitive subject with the purpose of representing reality and thus guiding action.

Thus, I am not at all hostile to McDowell's idea that spontaneity is necessarily involved in sense experience and that we cannot access a mere given that is not infused with traces of our own activity. My central thesis that experience is a response to sensory input looks very like McDowell's view "that experiences themselves are states or occurrences that inextricably combine receptivity and spontaneity," that they are "receptivity in operation."[7] I am even close to McDowell's claim that concepts function in experience from the very beginning, since I believe that a cognitive representation of reality is impossible without the involvement of some sort of ideal content in Bradley's sense. Why, then, would I take the time to challenge McDowell's argument? Is it merely

7 John McDowell, *Mind and World*, 24.

that I have scruples about having a position I agree with supported by an argument I cannot accept?

There is more to it than that. The thing is that the very idea of a concept covers a wide variety of cases. At one end we have the sort of concept that is closely connected to our language, and carries the meaning we can express through the use of some word. These representations, which endow words with their meaning and explain how different words (e.g. in different languages) may have the same meaning, may be called concepts in the strict sense. It is not necessary, of course, to restrict concepts in this sense to cases where we have an actual word. It is enough to have the concept formed so that we could *invent* a word to express it. Once concepts are introduced as the meanings of words, it is possible to have a penumbra of similar entities with which no word has as yet been associated. This allows for the development of language and the coining of completely new words.

At the other extreme, we have concepts that have no connection with language and whose function is merely to guide the activities of creatures endowed with purposes. It may well be that it is such lower-grade concepts that are involved in sense experience. Visual representations, for instance, provide a map of the environment that helps control our progress toward our objective although it does not involve a conceptual structure ready to be expressed in language.

Since justification is an operation that takes place at the level of language and associated mental states, McDowell's demand that our empirical beliefs be *justified* by our sense experiences will insert into experiences concepts of a higher type than is warranted, because this is required to warrant the empirical beliefs based upon them. In *Mind and World*, McDowell explicitly acknowledges "a demanding interpretation for words like 'concept' and 'conceptual'" (47). Thus, I have been attacking McDowell's argument to make room for a less intellectualized version of sense experience than McDowell has foisted upon us. Gareth Evans has introduced the idea of an informational system, within which perception forms a central division (the other divisions are communication and memory). This informational system "constitutes the substratum of our cognitive lives."[8] The deflection of McDowell's argument permits perceptual states to have an informational content that is not conceptual in the strict sense.

As we have already seen (chapter 8, section 4), "information" comes in two forms. There is the information contained in and transmitted by

8 *The Varieties of Reference*, 122.

physical systems and there is the information extracted through cognitive activity. The pattern of sensory stimulation generated by forces in the external world *contains* the information about the external world transmitted through the usual physical and physiological channels. This sensory input has an informational content, in the way in which a pattern of tree rings contains information about and represents the career of the tree over many years, which is causally responsible for the pattern. But sense experience does not merely *contain* the information transmitted by the sensory stimulation; at this level, we have *extracted* the information. The pattern of information contained in the sensory input may be distributed over many bearers of this information, but its extraction in sense experience must be carried out by a single subject. It is the unity of experience which shows that the information available within experience has been extracted, and this extraction of information takes place through the response of the subject to the manifold input coming into the system. It is perfectly clear that states may contain and transmit information without there being any participation of concepts. The controversial question is whether or not concepts are necessarily involved in the *extraction* of information by a cognitive subject.

It is not unreasonable to suggest that there are actually two distinguishable phases in our cognitive processing. There is an initial phase of sense experience in which the information extracted from the input is available to guide our behaviour and a more developed and specialized phase of conceptual thought proper in which the extracted information is being readied for communication and expression in language. This distinction explains the common feeling that sense experience is somehow richer and more detailed than the system of concepts – in the narrow sense – backing up the language we speak. For example, we seem to be able to experience and distinguish a great range of colour shades, which vastly exceed the small band of colour words – and their associated concepts – that we have available in our language.

John McDowell attempts to defuse this point by introducing a clever linguistic device – "one can give linguistic expression to a concept which is exactly as fine-grained as the experience, by uttering a phrase like 'that shade,' in which the demonstrative exploits the presence of the sample."[9] Even if we can use this device to bring *any* shade to concepts, it does not follow that it can be used on *all* the discriminable shades we experience at a given time. Even if we introduce a conceptual Paul Bunyan to perform feats beyond what we can normally credit, the fact remains that we

9 *Mind and World,* 57.

enjoy our colour experiences all the time, while conceptualizing particular shades in this way only in very special circumstances. There remains a distinction between the earlier phase of sense experience and a later stage at which elements may be conceptualized.

3 SCENARIOS

The content of sense experience is extraordinarily complex and detailed, especially if we consider the content of our dominant sense, which is the sense of sight. Moreover, the visual field, which is integrated in a more general perceptual field, has a definite structure. This structure has been recognized by Christopher Peacocke in his important notion of a "scenario."[10] A scenario is a form of representational content that involves the labeling of an origin and system of axes. In addition to the origin and system of axes, a scenario must specify a way of filling out the space around the origin. It must determine, for instance, where surfaces are to be found in relation to the origin through the use of the system of axes.

Since the scenario is a spatial *type,* the origin and axes will not be a specific place and set of directions in the real world. The origin and axes must be labeled by a set of interrelated properties. As an example, Peacocke suggests that "one kind of origin is given by the property of being the center of the chest of the human body, with the three axes given by the directions back/front, left/right, and up/down with respect to that center" (62). This may have some connection with a suggestion I made earlier that we are not just agents who can make changes in the world, but locomotives who can change our own position.

Because the scenario is a spatial type, in itself it is neither a correct nor incorrect representation of anything. The space around the subject will indeed be correctly described if it instantiates the spatial type, but for the scenario to be taken as such a description, it must be positioned in the here and now. We can imagine the nightmare depicted in the film *Groundhog Day* with Bill Murray, where the same stream of scenarios is experienced at the beginning of each day, but we take our present experience to represent the world today. As a representation of tomorrow and the next day we hope that it is incorrect.

If Peacocke is on the right track, we have here a more sophisticated way of dealing with the problem we encountered in chapter 7, section 6 in our quest for basic perceptual acts involving propositional content.

10 *A Study of Concepts,* chapter 3.

We came up against a dilemma when trying to describe what Hamlet saw when he discovered Polonius behind the curtain. Hamlet may have thought, and could have said, that he saw that there were feet protruding from underneath the curtain, but we disallowed this because the feet were encased in boots and had to be inferred. On the other hand, we cannot say that Hamlet saw that there were boots, because there is no evidence that the concept of boots was present in his mind at the time.

Using the scheme Peacocke provided, we can now take the basic perceptual act as the positioning of a scenario. The non-conceptual representational content defining the scenario could be taken as the foundation for the string of reports in ordinary language about what Hamlet saw. Such reports involve propositional content, because they indicate beliefs reached on the basis of the perceptual experience. There can be different reports because there can be different beliefs, involving a lesser or greater inferential component.

In chapter 9, section 2, I attempted to bridge the gap between sensation and cognition by conceiving sense experience not as mere sensation, but as a response by the subject to the sensory input in order to represent the world around. Peacocke's notion of a scenario fits in very nicely with this approach. The response of the subject to the sensory input may be the construction of a scenario organized in the way suggested. The organization of the scenario betrays the presence of an organizer, responding to the input in an aggressive fashion.

Another virtue of Peacocke's theory, from my point of view, is its emphasis on the spatial character of the scenario. I have argued that the representations constructed in response to the sensory input presuppose a reality that must be conceived as having parts. Distinctions in space (and time) seem a good way to provide the parts for the reality to be represented. The detail in the content of Peacocke's scenarios introduces the empirical differences within the object of representation

There is also a close connection between the scenarios of Peacocke and the maps I used to illuminate the nature of sensory representation in chapter 10, section 1. Maps are like scenarios writ large. Although a copy of a map as a piece of paper is a particular thing, the mapping of the environment it expresses has a universal character. Professional maps contain instructions about how the map is to be positioned, such as specifications of latitude and longitude, but rough sketch maps are more ambiguous. Nevertheless, the map must be positioned before its correctness can be evaluated (the insertion of the notation "You are here*" will help, but the orientation of the map must also be decided). Maps are a good model for understanding sensory representation precisely because they are an extension of the strategy we use in our scenarios.

Peacocke's approach, as we have seen, is well designed to handle the variety of reports about what a person perceived, where there is a greater or lesser degree of inferential supplementation on the part of the subject. But there is another complication illustrated by variations in what Peacocke calls "perceptual acuity" (63). In a given situation, there is a range of scenarios specifying ways of filling the space around the origin, corresponding to variations in the perceptual equipment of the subject. A man with poor vision has a fuzzier representation of the scene around him before he puts on his glasses. This undeniable fact puts a strain on Peacocke's neat exposition of a correctness condition for positioned scenarios. Peacocke writes that "the content given by the positioned scenario is correct if the scene at its assigned place falls under the scenario at its assigned time, when the scenario is positioned there in accordance with the assigned directions" (65). For Peacocke, the relation between the actual scene and a scenario it "falls under" is the relation of instantiation. This is certainly an improvement on the idea that the complete correctness of the scenario requires an exact matching between the positioned scenario and the scene. There is a range of states of the external world, varying in imperceptible details, consistent with the correctness of my visual representation.

To some extent Peacocke can handle variations in perceptual acuity in the following way. "Greater acuity corresponds to restriction of the set of ways of filling out the space whose instantiation is consistent with the correctness of the representational content" (63). Greater acuity is desirable, because the greater this restriction, the more information is provided. This idea works well enough within a normal range of acuity, but once acuity deteriorates below a certain point, e.g. through poor eyesight or poor conditions, it is uncomfortable to talk about correct representation. In the night, it is said, all cows look black, but can we say that the representation of the colour of the cow is correct because it is consistent with the cow being any colour when seen in the daylight?

Once a sensory representation is regarded not just as a particular that is an effect of antecedent causes but as a universal that permits instantiation, the big step has been taken. This account is very much in line with the distinction drawn by F.H. Bradley, who recognizes that the appearance present in immediate experience has two sides to it. "There is a 'what' and a 'that,' an existence and a content, and the two are inseparable."[11] Through an act of judgment, the ideal content of the experience is referred to the reality beyond. This act of judgment

---

11 See note 2, above.

corresponds to the act of positioning the scenario in reality, which is what introduces questions of correctness in Peacocke's theory.

This brings up a problem about which Peacocke does not have a great deal to say in *A Study of Concepts*, the question of how we access the reality in which we position our scenarios. A scenario that *can* be positioned correctly *must* be positioned correctly, if we are not to be led astray, as when we are deceived by mirrors or a mirage.[12] To position a scenario I must begin with an egocentric sense of space that supplies a structure in relation to the here and now. This structure is connected with the variety of my possible actions: I can move ahead, or I can stay where I am. Ahead is the direction in which my legs will take me if I begin to walk; if I am lying on my back, there is no ahead, but only above. If I turn around, the scenario that I initially positioned in front of me, I now position behind me. The combination of scenarios derived from the sensory inputs of the past and the present makes possible a representation of my complete environment. This will guide me both when I am moving forward and backing up. This tie-in between action and the egocentric space in which scenarios are positioned is recognized by Gareth Evans, for whom "an egocentric space can exist only for an animal in which a complex network of connections exists between perceptual input and behavioural output."[13]

There may be different scenarios associated with different senses, such as the sense of sight and the sense of touch, but the connection with action requires that they be co-ordinated. We all need good eye-hand co-ordination and a superior level of this skill confers distinct advantages. When this co-ordination breaks down, for example in the case of visual illusion, we are in trouble. For Gareth Evans "There is only one egocentric space, because there is only one behavioural space."[14]

Another presupposition of the egocentric sense of space is what Maurice Merleau-Ponty called the *embodiment* of the self. Unless the being enjoying the experiences and performing the actions has a particular place in nature, it will not be possible to give a meaning to the terms that presuppose such a centre in the here and now. We are now getting into waters both muddy and deep, and I shall pursue this line no further. For the theory of scenarios what is presupposed is some way of positioning

12 The trouble with dreams is that although we may enjoy scenarios that are quite detailed, we are not able to position these scenarios in the real world and hence cannot take effective action to remedy any difficulties.

13 *The Varieties of Reference*, 154. The entire section 6.3 from which this quotation is drawn is very illuminating. It ties in with my conception of myself as "locomotive man."

14 Ibid., 160.

these scenarios in an actual world; how this is done is a good question that I will make no further attempt to answer at this time.[15]

For Peacocke, the important theme is that the spatial type introduced in the scenario is a *non-conceptual* representational content. He is drawing an explicit contrast between the representational content available in sense experience and conceptual representations proper. There is no counterpart to this distinction in Bradley's theory. The question is whether it is possible to draw a line within the ideal content recognized by Bradley between concepts proper and a representational content that is not conceptual.

We may get what we need by exploiting a distinction I made in the preceding section between the kind of concepts that provide a backing for language and a lower-grade conceptual activity whose function is merely to guide and control our behaviour. It is easy enough to alter the description of the low-grade concepts thought to be involved in sense experience and turn them into a *non-conceptual* representational content. This can be regarded as no more than a change in terminology, because it preserves the distinction between the kind of concept associated with language and the representational elements in experience associated with behaviour.

Peacocke attempts to separate concepts proper from the spatial types he regards as non-conceptual representational contents by distinguishing the ways in which they are individuated. He argues that "a concept is ... individuated by the condition required for a thinker to possess it. A spatial type is not" (67). I am not sure what precisely this distinction amounts to and I am not sure that it works. In any event, an attempt to isolate the cluster of mental representations surrounding the use of language may have other problems, given a complication Peacocke himself introduced. This is the "need to recognize a kind of nonconceptual representational content in addition to the positioned scenario" (74).

The complication can be illustrated by the example of the square and the diamond.[16] The same figure can be perceived both as a regular diamond shape and as a square rotated from its standard orientation. The scenario is the same, with the same conditions of correctness, but the experiences are different. Peacocke explains this as "a difference in the way in which symmetries are perceived. When something is perceived as a diamond, the perceived symmetry is a symmetry about the bisectors

15 I have provided further discussion of Merleau-Ponty and the place of mind in nature in *Why Consciousness Is Reality*, chapter 6.

16 This example was originally discussed by Ernst Mach, *The Analysis of Sensations*, 106.

of its angles. When something is perceived as a square, the perceived symmetry is a symmetry about the bisectors of its sides" (76).

In explaining the difference between these perceptions, some very high-powered concepts have been employed. This in itself would not bother Peacocke since he argues, quite reasonably, that even if certain concepts are inevitably employed in the *descriptions* of perceptions and scenarios, it does not follow that these concepts are involved in the *constitution* of the perceptions. Nevertheless, something more than the bare scenario is clearly involved, since the scenario is the same, although the perceptions are different. What more there is, according to Peacocke, is "a second layer of nonconceptual representational content" (77). He calls these additional contents "*protopropositions*," and when "a protoproposition is part of the representational content of an experience, the experience represents the property or relation in the protoproposition as holding of the individual or individuals it also contains" (77).

These protopropositions look very like regular judgments or propositions, which is why they are called "proto*propositions*." The difference seems to be that the universals assigned to the individuals are not proper concepts, as defined by Peacocke. He calls them, instead, "properties and relations." But these universal properties and relations are hard to distinguish from the predicates in a judgment, which are normally considered to be universal concepts. Perhaps we should introduce "protoconcepts" to function as the predicates of protopropositions!

Protopropositions were invented to explain a change in perceptual experience not accompanied by a change in the scenario. But once protopropositions have been introduced, it is reasonable to suppose that they permeate through and through the scenarios that map the environment.[17] As a matter of terminology, it may be more elegant to drop the expressions "protoproposition" and "protoconcept" in order to use "proposition" and "concept" as generic terms to cover all cases. This would not preclude Peacocke from isolating a privileged *species* of proposition and concept, satisfying the constraints he sets out in his book, if he can make out a good case for so doing.

If the coverage of the expressions "proposition" and "concept" is extended in this way, perhaps we should consider a further extension so that a scenario is a concept in this wide sense, and the positioning of a scenario is a proposition in this wide sense. After all, a crucial aspect of a scenario is its generality, which permits its positioning – correctly or

---

17 This would appear to be in line with recent physiological research which has discovered, for example, clusters of neurons that function as edge detectors.

incorrectly – in a variety of places. I am prepared to argue, indeed, that the essence of a cognitive representation is this kind of generality. I count as a cognitive representation not just one that contains and allows the transmission of information, but a representation in which the information has been extracted through the activity of the cognitive subject. This means that the significant divide is between general representations that may function in cognition and mere particulars. An image as traditionally understood is a mere particular, unless the information it contains is extracted by the subject. This is exactly in line with Bradley's doctrine about the ideality of the content that functions in cognition. This view does not, of course, preclude the separating out of various sorts of cognitive representations with special features, such as the scenarios of Peacocke or the concepts, in the narrow sense, associated with the use of language. Nevertheless, the family connections among all forms of cognitive response to the environment must be maintained through the recognition of the generality which is involved.

4 PRIMITIVE COGNITION

The way in which the conceptual, in the wide sense, permeates sense experience can be better understood if we are prepared to make one final radical move. I have rejected the traditional view that we begin by conceptualizing the similarities and differences in our sensations and then make inferences to the character of the world beyond. This kind of move is possible only at a later stage in our intellectual development, when we are able to review our instinctive beliefs about the character of the external objects. I have not, however, challenged the framework within which the traditional empiricist view was developed, "that all our knowledge begins with experience."[18] I may indeed have rejected the traditional wisdom that the enjoyment of particular sensations is the first stage in the development of our cognitive life, with the introduction of concepts taking place in a second phase, on the back of a process of comparing and abstracting from the given particulars. But I have not so far denied that the foundation for our empirical knowledge lies in sense experience and perceptual consciousness, from which we somehow distill the concepts that figure in empirical knowledge. The change I have made is to recognize that sense experiences are created by the subject in response to the sensory input as representations of reality. Since these sensory representations have built into them a general character that

18 Kant, *Critique of Pure Reason*, B1.

allows them to be positioned in the domain of particularity that is the actual world, they have an affinity with general concepts, which will ease the transition from sense experience to conceptual thought. It is no longer necessary to introduce generality through a sense-datum theory that inserts a stage at which the subject forms concepts of given sensations.

I am now ready for a much more radical move. I wish to argue that the construction of sensory representations and scenarios is very far from being the first step in the development of cognition in living beings. On the contrary, the formation of our familiar sense experiences in response to sensory input is a special and evolved function for certain higher level cognitive beings. There is a stage in the evolution of life before sense experience as we know it appeared on the scene. In the case of human beings, visual sensations, for instance, must be supported by a functioning visual cortex and when the cortex is destroyed, the visual sensations are nowhere to be found.[19] Primitive life-forms with inadequate brains presumably do not have the wherewithal to constitute sensory representations of their environment.[20]

If such primitive creatures are nevertheless endowed with purposes, they must also have some form of cognitive representation of the environment that will guide them in the pursuit of these purposes. When I argued earlier that the purpose served by the construction of sensations was the representation of the environment, I was careful not to say that the environment could be represented *only* in this way. I left the door open for other forms of representation.[21]

To explain the nature of these other forms, we may perhaps exploit Peacocke's notion of "protoproposition." These protopropositions (and the "protoconcepts" they must contain) were introduced to account for differences in representational properties associated with the same scenario. If, as I suggested, these protoconcepts permeate the scenarios we construct, then they may well be of very ancient lineage, and may be operative in primitive agents who have not yet developed the capacity to construct sensory representations that would display the world around them and guide their behaviour. For such organisms to achieve their purposes, they must be guided by protopropositions and protoconcepts.

19 See chapter 1, section 4, on "blindsight."

20 One may even speculate that the very development of the brain is connected with the capacity to form a sensory map of the external world.

21 Using his vocabulary, I am agreeing with David Chalmers that not all representational properties are phenomenal properties, for much the same reasons. See *The Character of Consciousness*, 343–4.

If we adopt the proposal I made to extend the coverage of the term "concept" in a wide sense to include the protoconcepts, I can display my theory as a dramatic reversal of the usual empiricist position that sensations are primitive and concepts emerge when the higher function of the understanding is brought into play. I wish to stand this order of development upon its head and insist that concepts are more primitive than sensations. The use of general concepts to respond to the sensory input on which our knowledge of the environment must ultimately depend is a more primitive function than the construction of sensations or sensory representations. The proposal is that general concepts are original and necessary to cognitive life, whereas sensations emerge later. Sensations emerge when sophisticated percipients are able to form a kind of map of their environment, instead of reacting immediately to the incoming stimuli in accordance with their concepts and purposes.

This far-reaching proposal is indeed open to objection. The difficulty is that once we get to life-forms so primitive that we can be reasonably sure that they do not enjoy sensations, the behaviour is so simple that a purely mechanical explanation may appear completely satisfactory. What I have to assume is that there are beings whose behaviour cannot be explained mechanically without bringing in purposes and concepts, but which do not enjoy sensory representations of the kind enjoyed by the higher animals. My intuition is that there is a large domain of simple organisms, such as bacteria and viruses, which do not have sensory representations but which do not operate in a purely mechanical fashion. Once one has allowed purpose into the natural order in order to explain the behaviour of human beings, there is no great economy achieved by scrupulously restricting purposiveness to higher forms of life. Once purposes have been admitted, it may be legitimate to extend the notion to cover cases where an alternative mechanical explanation of behaviour is not implausible.[22] Even the humble virus may have its purposes, and although it does not enjoy sensations, it reacts to its environment to achieve its purposes, which involves general concepts. If concepts are there from the beginning, essentially involved with purpose and life, we are not faced with the hard problem of how they emerge.

This suggestion that conception is more basic than sensation, which is a special function of higher organisms, flies in the face of the entire philosophical tradition. It is a radical challenge to the ordering of sense and understanding that Plato originally set out in his diagram of the

---

22 I would draw the line, however, at things that are in some sense alive. I would not follow Aristotle in ascribing purpose to inanimate objects, explaining gravity in terms of the purpose of heavy things to make for the centre of the universe.

divided line, where understanding with its general concepts and forms is *above*, and sense, as a repository of particular sensations and images, is *below*. This translates into the position that only *higher* beings, often restricted to *human* beings, are capable of understanding, whereas the *lower* animals are confined to the level of sense.[23] An extreme form of the Platonic view is, indeed, widespread even today in the Wittgensteinian association of concepts with the use of language.[24] Since the use of language is virtually confined to human beings, only human beings, by and large, will have the power to form general concepts.

The words in the language of a society are typically and originally used to describe things in a public world, since this language can come into being only if there is reference to public objects to which different members of the linguistic group have access. Therefore, the development of this Wittgensteinian approach has brought about the eclipse of the traditional empiricist epistemology, in which our cognitive life begins with the conceptualization of our sensations and our beliefs about an external world are generated only through inference. I am endorsing the criticism of traditional empiricism for a totally different reason. We do not begin with judgments about sensations because at the beginning of our cognitive life there *are* no sensations. To get to the beginning of our cognition, we may have to go back, before birth, to the fetus. Before the fetus has been able to build up anything recognizable as sense experience, it is a purposeful creature with its own conceptual capacities. Wittgenstein introduces concepts at an extremely high level, after interpersonal relations have been established in a society; I am introducing concepts at an extremely low level, well before powers of sensory representation have been acquired. If such creatures enjoy purposes and the associated cognitive life, then their concepts will relate perforce to their external world, since there is no internal display of sensations to be characterized.

In the first section of the preceding chapter I argued that the conceptions involved in our cognition of the environment were available at different levels of generality, depending on our purposes. I argued the point on the basis of an examination of the high-level cognitive activity that can be assigned to human beings; but I see no reason to suppose that this distinction disappears when we move down to primitive organisms. One may speculate, indeed, that very primitive organisms use very

---

23 An ulterior motive for this Platonic picture was to reserve for human beings an immortal soul with access to the eternal forms Plato associates with concepts.

24 This is plausible only when the term "concept" is used in what I have called its narrow sense.

simple and abstract conceptual distinctions, such as the distinction between what it may feed on and what may feed on it, which will determine the direction of locomotion. As organisms become more complex, it is reasonable to suppose that there will be more complex distinctions within the information extracted from the environment.

The fundamentalist theory that pushes back the operation of concepts to the most primitive forms of purposive organisms does not, indeed, explain these concepts by revealing how they came into existence. Their arrival on the scene would appear to be connected with that poorly defined topic – the problem of the origin of life. At this point one may begin to feel the tug of panpsychist theories like that of Whitehead,[25] which involve the general (eternal objects) in the constitution of every actual entity, no matter how primitive.

I am well aware that there are many who would regard my assignment of conceptual activity to primitive organisms as both bizarre and gratuitous. A purely mechanical account of human life has its problems, because of the insistent facts of consciousness standing in the way. But there is nothing to interfere with a mechanical account of the behaviour of primitive organisms, unless we choose to invent it. Nevertheless, there is good reason to invent a cognition of reality below the level of sensory consciousness. For one thing, it explains how sense experience can function as a representation of reality guiding behaviour. It functions in this way because it has evolved in organisms that already have capacities to represent the reality in which they conduct their lives. It has evolved because this way of mapping reality is an improved system for achieving the purposes envisaged by the organism.

25 Cf. *Process and Reality,* (Cambridge University Press, 1929).

13

The Perception of the Future

1 THE CAUSE AND OBJECT OF PERCEPTION

I have argued that sense experience has been constructed by the subject as a representation of a reality structured in accordance with the forms of space and time. Since the sensory input is arriving from various quarters, the representation of reality will conform to this and the sensory map constructed will represent the different characters of different regions in space. We learn to build up a sensory representation of our world, normally with more detail for things that are close by.

Our world, however, is evolving all the time. What stage in its history do we represent in our perception? The thesis of this chapter is that the basic function of perception is to represent the future.[1] This goes against the commonsense view that we perceive the contemporary world, that we experience what is going on now at the present moment. The commonsense view is already under attack from the other side by those who are sensitive to the scientific account of the perceptual process; it seems that the objects of perception must lie in the past, normally the immediate past.[2] This "time-lag" argument, which overturns the commonsense view, depends, indeed, on the identification of the *object* of perception and the *cause* of perception. With this identification, the *object* of perceptual experience cannot be in the present, since the *cause* is definitely in the past.

---

1 This section makes extensive use of the paper "The Perception of the Future," which I delivered at the eighteenth World Congress of Philosophy in Brighton, England (1988).

2 There are, indeed, some cases where the object of perception lies in the very remote past, e.g. when it is a distant star.

There are, however, some well-known problems in the way of the simple identification of the cause and the object of perception.[3] For every sense experience there is a wide variety of antecedent factors causally responsible. When I look at a table, I have a visual experience produced by the light reflected from the surface of the table, by the pattern of stimulation in the retina, by a sequencing of nerve impulses passing along the optic nerve, and by many other things. Which of these factors is to be identified as the object of perception?

Given a choice from among these various causal antecedents we would certainly single out the table, or more strictly the state of the table, in the immediate past, which was involved in the reflection of the light that generated the perceptual experience, since we do not perceive the table's entire career from construction to firewood. But why choose this factor in preference to the others? One suggestion is that I choose the table because it is an object of interest. I am more interested in the table than in the changes in the rods and cones at the back of my eye, because the table is the thing with which I can physically interact. I can put things on the table; I can lean on the table; I can even sit on the table. Also, notice that the example began with my looking at the table. Why would I do that, unless I had some interest in the table?

Donald Davidson has advanced an ingenious theory of "triangulation," according to which the surface of the table has special status because it is the least remote causal factor common to the visual experiences of different members of the linguistic community.[4] It is the table that lies at the intersection of the various causal chains connecting the object with the experience of other observers as well as myself. It is the table that I talk about with other people who have no easy access to the rods and cones at the back of my eye.

When we are perceiving the medium-sized physical things that we so often take as the objects of our perception, there is indeed operating a personal version of the triangulation that Davidson has introduced. When we carry out observations of some specific object, we generate a variety of different causal chains that have their origin in the same thing. There are chains involving the stimulation of the eye by light reflected

3 This is, of course, a classical problem. Fritz Heider reports that he wrote his thesis on this topic in 1920, and shows that it interested both Alexius von Meinong and Bertrand Russell. *The Life of a Psychologist,* 35–7.

4 This view was advanced in his plenary address to the eighteenth World Congress of Philosophy in Brighton, England (1988). See also *Subjective, Intersubjective, Objective.*

from the surface of the object;[5] there are chains involving the sense of touch when we feel the object with the left hand and with the right hand and with other parts of the body; and there are many other causal chains giving information about the object.[6]

This use of a variety of causal chains to provide information about the object at their intersection is not a sporadic occurrence – it is central to our operation as active beings. The argument from personal triangulation is actually closely connected with my earlier argument from special interest. The apple I am interested in eating is revealed to me on the tree through the visual system. I reach out to grip it with my hand, which involves the sense of touch and a feedback from the haptic sensory system. A kind of internal triangulation is central to our normal *modus operandi*, since our detailed information about the environment comes largely from the sense of sight, whereas to deal with the things in the world we mainly use our hands and feet. The co-ordination of our visual system with other sensory systems, introducing objects at the intersection of these chains, is thus a normal feature of our cognitive life.

What I have done is to appropriate Davidson's own idea of triangulation in order to knock out one of the props supporting his general theory. The distinction between the cause and the object of perception can be handled without invoking his theory of linguistic triangulation, which assumes different people talking about the same thing. The objects I isolate at the intersection of the various sensory chains feeding me with information are, of course, available to feed information to other people through other causal chains. The objects of my perception are at the intersection of possible causal chains providing information to various observers. We can talk about the same things in the public world, because the objects of your perception are the same as mine. But I do not need to talk with other people to fix the object I say I perceive.

There is, of course, more behind Davidson's triangulation theory than the need to solve the special problem of the cause and the object of perception.[7] I cannot deal with the Davidson theory in the detail it

---

5 There are separate chains for each eye, but the contributions from each eye are actually integrated in the brain before the construction of the visual image.

6 When I made this suggestion to Davidson in a question at the plenary session of the eighteenth World Congress, he replied that these chains all end up in the same place in the perceiving subject. This is true enough, but do we not always need the same place to co-ordinate the results of a triangulation? Even in the model case where the surveyor triangulates a rock at the other side of the river to calculate how wide it is, the information from the two observations and about the distance between them must all pass through the brains of the surveyor and into his or her mind to solve the problem.

7 See, for instance, Claudine Verheggen, "Triangulating with Davidson."

requires at this time, although I will say that if my discussion of the private language argument in chapter 5 is accepted, Davidson's concerns will largely evaporate.

I have emphasized that our interest in the object at the intersection of the various sensory chains has little to do with the community to which we belong. The hungry man is not interested in the apple because everyone is talking about it. Once we bring in the interest of the experiencing subject, we change the focus dramatically. I am more interested in the table of the future than the table of the past, since it is the table of the future that will have a role to play in my various projects. It is on the table of the future that I propose to put down the book of the future that I am now holding in my hand. Thus, the perceptual experience constructed in response to the sensory input is directed to the representation of the immediate future and not the immediate past, even if the past is the source of the information employed. Since the object of sensory representation is in the future, it cannot be strictly identified with any of the causal factors, which are all in the past.

2 IMAGINATION

There is a natural reluctance to say that the future is actually perceived (apart from supporters of clairvoyance), but there is no such reluctance to say that the future can be imagined. We must be able to represent the future in some way; otherwise, we could not make the kinds of plans we do, which are essential for intelligent action. Moreover, this representation of the future is not a mere general concept, since the object of representation is a structured domain of particularity. Although the information that determines the detail comes from the past, the object of representation lies in the future.

We may call the faculty that makes this possible "imagination." For instance, we can imagine the future consequences of various courses of action. The commonsense view is that the future can be imagined but not perceived, but if we do allow in some sense the perception of the future, we can bring perception and imagination more closely together. Suppose a coin drops from my hand, rolls away, and disappears down a grating. I do not believe that the coin has disappeared from the world. I imagine it lying there underneath the grating and take steps to recover it. The coin I imagine underneath the grating is in the same world as the grating I say I perceive, and the object I perceive and the object I imagine belong to precisely the same system of objects – the difference lies in the mode of representation. In the case of perception the representation is normally more vivid and is being fed by current sensory input.

Now it is reasonable to suppose that the coin imagined is the coin of the future, the coin that will be lying there when I am able to get to it. It is also reasonable, given the connection between imagination and perception, to suppose that the grating perceived is also the grating of the future. Although the perceptual representation is fed by an input from the past, this does not prove that the object of representation is itself in the past. Another example that may help to confirm this kind of account comes from duck shooting. The approved technique is to look at, and point the gun towards, the spot where the duck will arrive. The duck will then run into the shot with which it is on a collision course.

In the main part of this work I have tended to describe the content of sense experience as sensation, in order to emphasize its connection with its causal antecedents. But once we recognize that the sense experience is a *response* to the incoming stimuli, it is equally appropriate to describe this content as a kind of image, to emphasize its representative function. The idiom is common enough – for example, psychologists describe the spot we perceive on a blank wall after looking at a bright light as an after-image, not an aftersensation. The image experienced is real enough, but there is nothing corresponding to it on the wall, not even on the wall of the future, which is the wall from which the deluded would attempt to wash off the spot with a damp cloth.

There is, of course, normally a big difference between the kind of mental image involved in visual perception and mental images in the ordinary sense, a difference Hume tried to capture with his distinction between impressions and ideas, which were "faint copies" of the impressions (eidetic images would be a rare intermediate case, with the same vividness as impressions, but without the same connection to the sensory input). When I imagine the coin beneath the grating, I can use some sort of mental image to help me, but before the coin disappears out of sight, I can imagine its future state using a current impression.

3 IMAGES AND SCENARIOS

The notion of the mental image as the content of perceptual experience is developed by Christopher Peacocke[8] in his sophisticated concept of the "scenario." The thesis that the object of perception may lie in the future also fits smoothly with the distinction Peacocke draws between the scenario and the positioning of the scenario. The scenario itself is no

---

8 See chapter 12, section 3. I did not use the notion of scenario in my World Congress paper, since it was not available at that time.

doubt a component in my present experience, but if it is to count as a representation and cognition, it must be positioned. There is nothing compelling us to restrict this positioning to the world of the present – indeed if it is to be a useful guide for future behaviour, it must be positioned in the future. To guide my steps, I represent the bridge I must cross to get to the other side. What is important is to represent a bridge that will still be there when I get to it. The positioning of the scenario in the future is a necessary component in the planning process.

My argument that we perceive the future is perhaps not truly incompatible with our ordinary belief that we perceive a contemporary world. The ordinary person does not work with an exact concept of simultaneity. For common sense the present world is the world in which effective action can be taken, as opposed to the world in which it is now too late to act. The world in which I can act is the world I have identified as the world of the future.

My detailed representation of the world of the future must be based on information arriving from the past. I am prepared to position the scenario I construct in response to this sensory input in the future because of my faith in the general stability of my environment. My representation of the future on the basis of an input from the past is generally successful because of the actual level of constancy[9] in the physical universe. Without this constancy of things, the representational system of perception would not work and would never have developed as a guide to action. The system, of course, does not work perfectly, and we are sometimes misled by our mental maps. At one extreme, there is the rare case of total hallucination, where the map is completely fictitious. There are also the more frequent cases of minor distortion, where we are deceived by an illusion.

4 THE PERCEPTION OF EPISODES

The distortions I have mentioned are difficulties for every theory, but there is also a class of phenomena that pose special difficulties for the theory that we perceive the future. What about the perception of episodes, as when we experience a flash of lightning or the fall of an apple? Here the sensory stimulation is providing us, not with a map of the future, but with a *fait accompli*. To handle these cases, I make a distinction between the *perception of the environment* and the *perception of episodes*. The

9 I am deliberately using Hume's term.

perception of the environment is the representation of the future theatre of action, whereas the perception of episodes is the representation of what has taken place in the past.

In the case of the perception of episodes, such as the fall of an apple from a tree, the scenario is constructed after the apple reaches the ground, so that it must represent what has happened in the immediate past. It is worth noting that in cases like this, the scenario is no mere snapshot of the contemporary scene; it is a moving picture, involving transition. Even when there is no internal transition distinguished within the episode, we represent in perception what is over and done with. When I hear the sound of a hammer hitting a nail on the head, I do not register it as the sound it is, until it has stopped. There is a kind of time lag between the event and the experience that has nothing to do with the time it takes to feed the information from the incoming stimulus through the nervous system to the centre of consciousness.

The scenario theory has no problem with this kind of case. If we can position scenarios in the future, surely we can also position scenarios in the past. If the scenario involves transition, it must of course be assigned to an extended period in the past in order to represent what has happened in the past. The idea that we can perceive only what is strictly contemporary is not compatible with the perception of events that require time to complete. The problem disappears, if we allow the perception of past events. This information about the past supplies a basis for empirical inference from the past to the future, and hence is useful for guiding our behaviour in a less direct way. The mistake is to suppose that the representation of the future always depends on this kind of empirical inference. On the contrary, this kind of empirical inference can take place only in a context in which the future is already represented. Through causal reasoning the experience of episodes may lead us to modify the beliefs built into the perception of the settled state of the future. I plan my walk through the valley below the dam on the basis of how I perceive it will be when I get there. When I notice that the dam is collapsing, I have to alter my beliefs and my plans. This is not unlike the way in which the observation of the different effects of substances that look the same may alter the natural beliefs built into the perception that they are the same.

The revolutionary thesis of this chapter is that the central function of perception is to represent the theatre of action upon which I shall be called to perform in the future. This involves positioning in the future the scenarios I construct. This does not preclude me, however, from positioning the very same scenarios in the immediate past. When there is a perception of *events*, the scenario must be positioned in the past. In the case of the falling apple, there is indeed a difference between the scenario positioned in the past, which has the apple falling through the air, and the scenario positioned in the future, which has the apple lying on the ground. But when no change is taking place in the world, the scenarios positioned in the past and the future will be essentially the same.

The elaboration necessitated by the perception of episodes may allow us to bring back the perception of the contemporary world. If we represent the immediate past and the immediate future in the same way, surely we must form the same representation of the present that the world must pass through on its way from the past to the future. We may even form the idea of a kind of specious present, incorporating the immediate past and the immediate future. It is in this specious present that we represent the flight of the duck, including both information about the past and anticipation of its future course. I am happy to allow these qualifications of the original uncompromising doctrine, so long as it is conceded that the central purpose of perceptual experience is the representation of the future world in which we are called to perform.

A paradigm of perception I have endeavoured to replace in this work may be a source of resistance to the idea that we perceive the future. This is the notion that sense experiences are the ways the objects of perception appear to us. These appearances are, of course, subject to the conditions of observation involved. Now it is natural to think that the things that appear exist at the very time they appear. This is confirmed by the ordinary language idiom from which the concept of "appearing" has been taken. If something does not exist any longer, it may have appeared in the past but it does not appear any more. In the same way, the things that appear cannot be the things of the future, because they do not yet exist. The things of the future may appear in the future, but they cannot appear at the present moment.

This obstacle to perceiving the future disappears if we change the paradigm. Instead of construing sense experiences as the ways the objects appear, let us change to conceiving sense experiences as the ways in which we *represent* these objects. When the representative theory of perception replaces the theory of appearing, it makes perfect sense to say that in perception we form representations of the stage on which we are about to act – which is, of course, in the future. Not that the representative theory mandates that in perception we must represent the world of the future, but it makes this possible. Unlike the theory of appearing, the representative theory of perception has the flexibility to cover a variety of cases.

Thus, the argument of this chapter regarding the perception of the future confirms the general representative theory I have been supporting in this work. It also confirms the important suggestion, which I made earlier, to prevent the *object* of cognition from collapsing into the *act* of cognition. If the object of perception is in the future, it is necessarily distinct from the act of perception, which is in the present.[10]

10 Chapter 11, section 6.

Additional Ideas

BY THE END OF THE LAST CHAPTER, my explanation of the acquisition of perceptual knowledge is essentially complete. There are, however, a number of topics well worth exploring that emerge from my account, which I shall collect together in this final chapter. In the various sections, I examine the function of perceptual systems investigated by James J. Gibson; attempt to clarify the robust conception of the subject, self, or ego, which is a central presupposition of this work; show how my position can illuminate the fight between internalism and externalism; and discuss a recent theory put forward by David Chalmers.

1 JAMES J. GIBSON

In his important book *The Senses Considered as Perceptual Systems*, James J. Gibson has provided a plausible explanation of how it is that the flow of information through the senses from the ambient universe discloses the objects we normally assume we perceive. Granted that the information transmitted has no special connection to the processes in the brain that we may assume constitute the last stage in the information transfer, why do we focus on the things we do? Why do we take the information that we extract to be about things like tables and chairs, which are, after all, a quite remote cause of the relevant activity in the brain? This is the very question I raised in the previous chapter and tried to settle by invoking triangulation and the interests and concerns of the percipient subject.

Gibson answers the question by shifting attention away from what he calls "the passive receptors that respond each to its appropriate form of energy" (2). It is not that he denies that there is "a receptor mosaic for each sense connecting with the central nervous system and projecting the pattern of excited receptors to the brain" (4). The problem is that the sensory input and the physiological processes it engenders are changing all the time. The mass of information produced might very soon overload the cognitive system. What saves the day is that "certain higher-order variables of stimulus energy – ratios and proportions, for example – do *not* change. They remain invariant with movements of the observer and with changes in the intensity of stimulation" (3). The suggestion is that it is the information extracted from these invariances that informs about the physical objects we normally think we perceive.

Gibson takes the argument one step further. He believes that the various sensory systems we employ have been designed to detect invariances and to foster the pick-up of information from the environment. "The perceptual systems, including the nerve centers at various levels up to the brain, are ways of seeking and extracting information about the environment from the flowing array of ambient energy" (5).

The higher-order invariances introduced by Gibson would seem to be connected with the different levels of generality in concepts, which I discussed in the last section of chapter 12. For example, as I move towards a house, approaching from the front, my experience is changing all the time, with the front surface of the house occupying an ever larger proportion of the visual field (this will involve the progressive occlusion of what appears behind the house). What does not change is the ratio between the front door and the front of the house. Paradoxically, the relative size of these things has an absolute value, and is built into my concept of what the house is. The special point that Gibson makes is that the more general concept is extracted from the *flow* of information. It is such concepts that describe the familiar objects of our external world.

It may appear that to bring in Gibson's theory at this point is a bit of a flourish, introducing an exotic psychological theory into a philosophical account of perception (I call Gibson's theory "exotic" because what he calls his "ecological" approach is very far from being the standard method in the psychology of perception). Yet Gibson's theory is, in fact, exactly what I need to tie together the two parts of this book.

The first part of the book provided a qualified defence of the traditional theory of perception by introducing a second pass, in which we use judgments about our sensations and experiences to justify or correct our original empirical beliefs. This pattern of argument, however, presupposes empirical beliefs about an external world which must be originally acquired in some other way. In the second part of the book, I have endeavoured to show how our original beliefs about the environment are formed by the response of the cognitive subject to the incoming stimuli. Gibson's theory contributes to this explanation by showing how we extract values for higher-order variables from the flow of information coming from the ambient array. Such an extraction of values for higher-order variables can take place within the flow of sense experiences available in full consciousness, but there is no reason why it should not also take place in the primitive cognition discussed in chapter 12, section 4, which explained the phenomenon of blindsight.[1] The values extracted may be taken to correspond to the concepts used in judgment to capture the familiar objects of our external world.

In addition to the higher-level information, which does not change with a change in the conditions of information, there is also information fed in through the special senses, which *does* change. It is *this* information that provides the basis for the judgments about the exact nature of our sense experience used in the second pass. We can use a series of photographs from various angles to identify the object involved. In the same way we can infer from a set of experiences, each conditioned by its particular perspective, the thing which is their common cause. The information extracted for the cognition of each separate experience is more specific than the higher-order information employed in our original rapid response to the sensory input. This makes possible the review of our original beliefs in a second pass, which lies at the heart of the traditional causal representative theory of perception.

The fact is that the cognitive subject does not extract all the information being fed in through the sensory system – a selection is made. It is this selective feature that explains how we are able to make *both* our original judgments about things in the external world *and* judgments about our own sense experiences in the second pass.[2] What we may call, in Kantian terms, judgments of outer sense and judgments of inner sense involve different selections of information, because of the different purposes lying behind the two types of judgment. Once we have available, as explained in chapter 11, an a priori domain of space and time in which to posit objects and events, we can extract from the changing flow of information constancies suitable for characterizing such things. This is, indeed, the primary use of our cognitive faculties, because of our supreme interest in determining the nature of the environment in which we have to conduct our lives.

Making the selection that serves this interest does not, however, preclude making a different selection when our concern is to describe the course of our experience. This selection emphasizes the peculiarities of the special senses and the changes in the information flow. For example, when we are moving forward through a field of objects in front of

---

1 Blindsight is discussed in chapter 1, section 4.

2 It is these different selections which explain the different attitudes of the vulgar and the learned, to use David Hume's terms.

us, there are constancies in the information flow that make possible judgments about the settled nature of these objects. But there are also changes in the flow of information that reveal the changing character of the subjective experience associated with the movement of the perceiving subject.

2 THE ORIGIN OF THE SELF

One feature of this work that may disturb some readers is my confident introduction of a complex being who is both the subject of experience and cognition and an agent determined to change the world.[3] This being I identify with my innermost self and I assume that there are other similar beings associated with the human bodies I see around me. But what is this being and where does it come from? Ruling out the proposal that this special being is magically inserted into the flow of nature by a supernatural cause, the most common suggestion is that the experiencing subject somehow emerges from a sufficiently complex physical system, such as the human brain. Even if the emerging novelty is considered to be more than a mere new function of the complex system, I do not feel that this will be enough for my purposes, and wish to propose a different account.

According to this account, my origin as a unique individual came from the merger of a sperm from my father and an egg contributed by my mother. The resulting single-celled organism is the earliest version of my self. Before long, following the usual story, the cell divides and becomes two. My suggestion is that when this happens, the unity controlling the original cell does not necessarily disappear. It may remain behind to supervise the emerging two-celled organism. When it does disappear, so that there are two independent cells, perhaps this is when we get identical twins!

The idea is that in the standard case, when the original cell divides, we do not get two things in place of one, but three. We have the two daughter cells, but they are connected to one another in virtue of the unity of the original cell from which they are descended. As the organism develops the cells in the system become more numerous, and the corresponding self controlling the development becomes more complex and sophisticated. My suspicion is that the kind of consciousness with which we are familiar from the inside is gradually acquired by the subject in step with the development of the cerebral cortex.

---

3 I am leaving aside other possible aspects of this being, such as feelings and emotions.

This is no more, of course, than a highly speculative sketch of a possible theory. In a complete theory, there would have to be some account of how some cells, such as those forming the nails and the hair, seem to escape the immediate control of the central directorate and others, such as dead cells on the surface of the skin, are eventually eliminated from the system entirely. There are many, many problems that such a theory would have to solve.

The theory begins, moreover, by presupposing a special unity in the original cell that controls the manifold within it. I have not explained the nature of this unity, but if I am given a blank cheque, it might be a good idea to build into it a primitive form of cognition and purpose to make it easier to explain the developed forms of these functions, which are to be found in the mature self. The problem of life is essentially this problem of the special unity through which the cell combines its manifold. This is certainly a mystery – but isn't the origin of life regarded as a bit of a mystery by most people?

The reason I am making this suggestion is merely to indicate a possible source of the robust unity that I require for the centre of consciousness, cognition, and agency, without having it emerge at some point from a sufficiently complex and energetic system of neurons. At the present time, I do not foresee a great future for the attempt to develop the theory in greater detail; but the general idea is there to offer an alternative to the view that the subject and the self arises once the neural activity in the brain has attained a critical mass.

3 EXTERNALISM AND INTERNALISM

The theory outlined in this book may gain confirmation when we consider the solution it can offer to a worrisome problem that has divided philosophers into opposing camps. The problem is the conflict between externalism and internalism. There are certainly some states of mind, such as "feeling sad," which appear completely determined by the character of the person involved. Internalists believe that all psychological states are of this kind. Externalists get their chance, because there are also some states of mind whose definition appears to involve objects which lie outside the mind (and even outside the body) of the person to whom these states are assigned. A particularly important class of such states is formed by beliefs. John believes that Fido is a hairy dog. To specify the content of John's belief, we must introduce the animal called "Fido," whose characteristics will make the statement that Fido is a hairy dog true, if it is, or false, if it is not. Now, if the content of John's belief necessarily involves an external object, then there is no way John's psychological state can be identified with a complex of physiological states, which by definition do not involve anything outside the body. This means that reductive materialism is untenable. A discourse that refers to objects outside the body cannot be reduced to a discourse that does not.

Although it may be convenient to identify a person's beliefs by specifying the objects to which the person refers, there are reasons to think that it is not these actual objects that constitute the essential content of these beliefs. Suppose that the Fido John believes to be a hairy dog is not a dog at all, but a strange-looking rabbit. If I discovered that Fido is a rabbit, I might now, from my own superior point of view, classify John's belief as a belief about what is, in fact, a rabbit, but this would not change in any way the actual content of John's belief. If Fido had turned out to be a funny rabbit, this would make false John's belief that Fido was a dog, but there would be no change in its content. The content has to stay the same, if the original belief is to be rejected as false. There is an even more extreme case where Fido does not exist at all, but has been introduced into discourse through a set of peculiar hallucinations. Even on this assumption, John's belief does not change, only its cognitive status.[4]

The first problem for externalism, then, is that a belief might be exactly the same, even if it picked out different objects in different circumstances – a hairy dog or a funny rabbit. The second problem is in a way the opposite of the first, for here we have *different* beliefs that ascribe the same property to the same thing. This problem arises because the objects to which the subject refers must be introduced through some mode of representation. It is perfectly possible for the same object to be introduced through *different* modes of representation.[5] For example, an author may introduce variety by referring to Aristotle as The Stagyrite, The Peripatetic, or The Founder of the Lyceum.[6] It is also possible for someone to use different ways of representing the same thing without realizing that it is the same thing that is referred to. This is the point of the example, used by Kripke, about Pierre and London/Londres. Since Pierre does not understand that London and Londres are the same city, he can happily maintain what are from the externalist point of view contradictory beliefs about the city that he is representing in these different ways.[7]

---

4 This would, of course, be denied by Hilary Putnam in his fantasy about Twin Earth. See "The meaning of 'meaning,'" 131–93.

5 This is, of course, closely related to Frege's point that signs may have the same meaning but different senses. The expressions "the morning star" and "the evening star" have different senses, but they mean or refer to the same object.

6 See Joseph Owens, *The Doctrine of Being in the Aristotelian Metaphysics.*

7 S. Kripke, "A Puzzle about Belief."

The *internalist* theory, then, depends on the crucial assumption that the objects to which we refer in empirical discourse must be introduced through some mode of representation. Once this is granted, it is easy to see that in different circumstances, the same mode of representation may introduce different objects, just as the same personal pronoun "I" will *refer* to different people when it is *used* by different people. Also, different modes of representation may introduce the same object, just as different proper names may refer to the same person, whether or not this is realized by the speaker.[8]

A well-formed belief of a certain basic kind[9] involves reference to an object together with a description of that object. To have beliefs about a specific object requires that one think about that object, which involves some mode of representation that singles out this particular thing. The mode of representation does not have to be a linguistic expression, although the use of language is standard procedure when one wants to indicate what one is thinking about to other people. Even when I want to convey what I have in mind to other people, language is not absolutely necessary – sometimes a grunt or a gesture will do! Certainly, beliefs expressed in language are easier to talk about and I believe that the points I want to make can all be made while restricting myself to this special subclass.

Suppose I want to report to Tom – or people in general – Mary's belief that the cat is on the mat. Usually, the simplest way to do this is to repeat *verbatim* what Mary has said: "The cat is on the mat." But there are other times when this would not be the best strategy. Mary knows that the cat she is talking about is her own cat "Fluffy," but how will Tom know this, unless I tell him? To convey Mary's belief to Tom I may have to paraphrase what she actually said. Mary says: "Fluffy is on the mat." I report to Tom: "Mary believes that her cat is on the mat."

Sometimes, indeed, in reporting Mary's belief I may use a description of a person involved that is not available to Mary. Mary believes that her neighbour has left for Brazil, having seen him carry to a taxi a large suitcase labeled RIO DE JANEIRO. Mary knows the man as her neighbour, but not as the President of the Excelsior Financial Corporation. Tom knows the man as the President of the Corporation, in which he has invested heavily, but not as Mary's neighbour. Therefore, I say to Tom:

8 This corresponds quite closely to the distinction between sentences and the statements they are used to make drawn by Sir Peter Strawson in *Introduction to Logical Theory*, e.g. 3–4.

9 I have in mind the basic structure in the logic of *Principia Mathematica*, expressed by the form "Fa." Other types of belief will require a more complicated account.

"Mary believes that the President of the Excelsior Financial Corporation has left for Brazil." Other times, to report the nub of Mary's belief, I may even have to *correct* Mary's description of the principal player. Quite apart from correcting slips of the tongue and other trivial errors, from time to time I may have to put right a serious distortion when passing on Mary's information. Suppose Mary has got it into her head that a man she once saw in an imposing uniform is a general. Mary tells me: "I saw the general at the market this morning." I have discovered that the man Mary thinks is a general is really the doorman at the Ritz-Carlton. In relaying Mary's information to Tom, therefore, I say: "Mary believes that she saw the Ritz-Carlton doorman at the market this morning."

This is, no doubt, the correct thing to say, if I realize that Tom and other police officers are interested in piecing together an account of the doorman's movements during the morning. Nevertheless, I am bound to have misgivings about the changes I have made, if I am concerned to remain faithful to the actual content of Mary's belief. These ambivalent concerns have caused confusion among philosophers studying the nature of belief. On the one hand, we are anxious to put together a large store of information about the objects in our environment, based on observations drawn from a wide variety of sources. For this purpose, the ways in which these objects are conceived by those who provide the information is not relevant, so long as there is no confusion about what the objects are. The construction of this integrated system of beliefs is what supports the *externalist* account of belief. On the other hand, the objects that figure in these beliefs cannot be introduced except through some mode of representation, and this is the basis for the *internalist* theory.

When I consider the beliefs of other people, normally, I am able to assume that the ways in which these other people represent the objects introduced in their beliefs are more or less the same as the ways in which I represent these same objects. The trouble begins in the rare cases where the modes of representation come apart, where I am not able to take over the way of representing the object used by the other person, either because it is a definite *misrepresentation* of the object, or because it will not help to identify the object in question for the third parties to whom I wish to communicate the belief. Beliefs that assign the same property to the same object may therefore be different beliefs, when different modes of representation are involved. Thus, the exact nature of a belief to be assigned to a particular person cannot be specified without determining the internal representation through which the object is introduced, which is what the internalist believes.

I can, however, favour the internalist theory without running the risk of having states of belief reduced to mere physiological states, because the representation of specific objects takes place under the aegis of the a priori concept of reality, which is a function different in kind from functions of a purely physiological nature. States of belief are internal to the cognitive subject and do not involve essential relations to real objects beyond themselves (there is always the logical possibility that the object intended does not exist). But on the other hand, they are not mere subjective states, because their general form is expressed through the concept of the reality beyond the act of belief. As Bradley has argued, acts of judgment (associated with beliefs) involve a reference to a reality beyond the act. Acts with this structure cannot be identified with mere physiological processes.

By using Bradley's account of judgment, we can see in general how to reconcile the truths of both externalism and internalism. But a more focused understanding can be reached by going to the version of objective idealism developed by C.A. Campbell (already introduced at the end of chapter 11, section 4). In the quoted piece[10] Campbell is concerned to evaluate the idealist thesis that the objects of our knowledge are not things in themselves but are determined at least in part by the character of the knowing mind. He resolves the problem by distinguishing between two senses of "object." By "object" we may mean "that particular part of the presupposed independent reality which in our judging activity at any particular moment we are seeking to know" (240). Alternatively, by "object" we may mean "that same part of the presupposed independent reality *in the character which it bears for our present cognition*" (240). The first sense of "object" is introduced in virtue of Bradley's basic thesis that an independent reality is presupposed in the very act of judgment, together with Campbell's proviso that this independent reality must be represented as having parts.[11] Objects in the second sense are introduced when we characterize certain parts of the presupposed independent reality "through a complex of ideal meanings"[12] (240). Objects determined through such characterizations are not mind-independent, and may not even exist. The dagger Macbeth saw before him wasn't really there, but we assume that some reality was there, not correctly represented as a

---

10 "The Mind's Involvement in 'Objects': An Essay in Idealist Epistemology," in *In Defence of Free Will*. This paper was originally a contribution to *Theories of the Mind*, a volume edited by Dr Jordan M. Scher and published in 1962 by the Free Press of Glencoe, a Division of the Macmillan Company.

11 In chapter 11, section 4, I suggest that the *parts* of reality are most easily understood in terms of a spatio-temporal structure.

12 This "complex of ideal meanings," as well as "the character which it [the object] bears for our present cognition," are what I have called "modes of representation."

dagger. The reason for the non-existence of the dagger was that all the available space was taken up by other objects, including a dagger-shaped volume of empty air where the dagger was supposed to be.

4 DAVID CHALMERS AND THE CHARACTER OF CONSCIOUSNESS

In concluding this book, it will be useful to compare and contrast the theories I have outlined with the views David Chalmers expressed in his recent book *The Character of Consciousness*. This should be particularly illuminating, because we are basically on the same side. We are both supporters of what Chalmers calls *Phenomenal Realism*. This is the view that we are aware of what it is like to have experiences, such as an experience of red, and that what we are aware of cannot be explained or reduced in purely physical terms.

The Character of Consciousness gets down into the trenches and fights a determined battle against the forces of contemporary materialism. The argument is detailed and careful and convincing. But even if the materialist option is eliminated and its supporters disappear, this is not the end of the matter. There is still much to be explained, even if we are now equipped with purely mental items, which the materialists could not permit.

In his earlier book *The Conscious Mind*, Chalmers distinguished between the Easy Problem and the Hard Problem. The Easy Problem was to explain in functionalist terms intentional states such as beliefs. The Hard Problem was to get rid of the insistent facts of consciousness, such as what it is like to experience red. In the earlier book, Chalmers was willing to concede to his opponents the functionalist analysis of intentional states in order to make them face the problem that there was no way to get rid of or reduce conscious experience. Now, he takes the view that matters are not that simple. Our immediate experiences are essentially involved in at least some of our beliefs, so that these beliefs are no more explicable in purely functionalist terms than the experiences themselves. "When we think and perceive, there is a whir of information processing, but there is also a subjective aspect" (3). When I perceive that the light has turned red, the redness I directly experience is essentially involved, either as a property of the traffic light (naive realism) or as a sensation produced in me (Locke and his friends). In any event it is clear that Chalmers is no longer prepared to allow the study of consciousness and intentionality to proceed in two independent streams. The interface between consciousness and intentionality has moved to the centre (339–41).

Chalmers develops this insight as the problem of the connection between the phenomenal and representational properties of mental states,
or cognitive subjects. He assigns representational properties to mental
states through a distinction between the veridical and the nonveridical.[13]
This distinction requires that the mental states have conditions of satisfaction that constitute the representational content of the state. The
state is veridical if and only if the conditions of satisfaction are satisfied.
For Chalmers, phenomenal and representational properties are normally integrated, so that states with the same phenomenal properties will
share the same representative properties and *vice versa*. He concedes
some exceptions on the fringes, such as blindsight, where we have representation without the presence of phenomenal character, but there does
seem to be a core of standard cases where this is plausible. If this is correct, and there is no possible reductive explanation of the phenomenal
properties, there will also be no reductive explanation of the representational properties.[14]

This is an approach with which I have considerable sympathy.
Chalmers' question about the relation between the phenomenal and the
representational properties of mental states does seem to correspond to
a central problem in my own discussion: "How do we move from the description of sense experiences as sensations belonging to the space of
causes to an account of the empirical knowledge associated with these
sensations, which belongs to the space of reasons?" My answer was that
the sense experiences are constructed by the subject in response to the
sensory input with the purpose of representing the environment. The
function of the construction of the sensations is to contribute to our
empirical knowledge of the external world.

Although it looks as if sense experience, by its very nature, has as its
purpose the representation of reality, this does not mean that we can
necessarily line up particular sense experiences with our ordinary beliefs
about the external world. We may begin with a hope that we can identify
a sensation, described through its phenomenal property, with a perceptual act characterized through its representational content. As explained
in chapter 7, however, the precise content of a perceptual act, supposed
to be associated with a given sense experience, is hard to pin down. It is
tempting to posit such acts of perception, because of the prevalence in

13 I refuse to join Chalmers in using the ugly word "falsidical."

14 This distinction between the phenomenal and representational properties of experiences is uncannily close to Bradley's distinction between psychological ideas and logical
ideas. For Bradley, it is the logical ideas that are "referred elsewhere" and thus function as
representations. See above, chapter 12, section 1: "Ideal Content."

ordinary language of idioms using verbs of perception such as "see," followed by a propositional construction. The trouble is that this idiom is not designed to isolate the content of a supposed perceptual act – it is used to indicate *beliefs* reached (largely) on the basis of visual input, but involving contributions from other sources. Attempts to pare away what was supplied from elsewhere, leaving behind the exact content of the act of *perception*, were not successful.

This is not unexpected if the account of primitive cognition developed in chapter 12, section 4 is accepted. According to this account, conscious sense experiences were originally developed in creatures who already enjoyed cognitive representation of their environment. The sense experiences could be constructed to function as maps, because they were embedded in a representational context. If we have the same sensations in a different context, with a different background,[15] our representation of the world may also be different.

Nevertheless, it remains true that visual experience, for instance, provides us with a kind of map of the external reality, and not just a meaningless design. The map is a good map if it represents things as they are. The commonsense idea is that we get the colours right in our visual map if the associated things in the world have colours that *resemble* colours in our map. Chalmers introduces the idea of an Eden before the Fall of Man where our experiences always get things right (381-2). In Eden, what we see is what is there. We are well aware, however, that we do not live in Eden. We sometimes see what is not there and things are not always as they appear. Nevertheless, the ideal of Eden may serve as a criterion of correctness for experience. We sometimes see colours that are not really there, as in the case of an afterimage. But in normal cases, it is supposed that the colours we see really are out there in the natural world, just as they are in Eden. The conditions of satisfaction built into the representation are satisfied and the experience is considered veridical.

This is the way ordinary people work, and for most of the time, we are all ordinary people. Trouble begins when those whom Hume calls the "learned" begin to poke around. This takes place when we see the possibility of extending the method of improving our discrimination of the objects we perceive by studying their effects on other things. The special move is to treat our *sense experiences* as effects produced by the external objects. This move becomes mandatory once scientific investigation reveals the chain of causes and effects conditioning perceptual experience.

15 The background I have in mind is closer to what John Searle calls the Network. He reserves his concept of the Background for nonrepresentational capacities. See *Intentionality*, e.g. 65-71.

For perception to be called veridical, it is no longer necessary that the rose have a property the same as the red colour we experience. So long as similar sensations are produced by similar things in the external world, we will be able to use causal inference to group together external objects as the same kind of thing.

Notice, indeed, that it does not follow automatically that the sensations produced in us do *not* resemble their external causes. It is perfectly coherent to claim that in some cases, and in *these* cases, effects do resemble their causes. We cannot rule out the possibility, for instance, that the rose has a colour that closely resembles the sense experience it produces in us.[16] We may very well want to say that the way we structure visual experience resembles, even if it fails to replicate, the layout of objects in the physical world. But in the case of colours and other secondary qualities, there are very good *empirical* reasons for favouring Locke's story.

Chalmers is sensitive to these considerations and proposes to handle them by introducing what he calls "a two-stage view of phenomenal content" (404). This view looks rather like the two-pass account I adopted. We begin in much the same way and offer very similar accounts of the first stage and the first pass. At the level of common sense, those whom Hume calls the "vulgar" take as veridical sense experiences where external things really do have the colours, smells, and tastes directly experienced. We can say that there are conditions of satisfaction that are satisfied in the case of veridical experiences, but not satisfied when experiences are nonveridical and illusory. These conditions constitute the representative content of the experiences. The trouble is that if Locke and his scientific friends are right, the conditions of satisfaction are never satisfied in the case of colours and other secondary qualities. This would mean that our experiences of colour, etc., are never veridical. My strategy was to save the *truth* of the statements through which we assign particular colours to objects by changing what it *means* for an object to be a certain colour. The rose is no longer red because it has the red colour I experience spread on its petals, but because it has the *power*, in suitable circumstances, to produce a certain kind of experience in the perceiver.[17]

Chalmers makes a more radical move. Leaving unchanged the phenomenal character of the experience, he changes its conditions of satisfaction and its representational content. The vulgar have a concept of illusion, and a distinction between veridical and nonveridical experiences,

16 Chalmers also makes this point on 410.
17 See chapter 3, section 4.

that allows the philosophers among them to introduce the idea that the experience has a representational content distinct from its phenomenal character. When we look at a blue door, we represent the door as having the very blue colour that we experience. There are conditions that must be satisfied if the representation is to be veridical. These conditions form the *content* of the representation.[18]

This account makes sense at the level of the vulgar, where the content is the actual blueness of the door. This is the condition that must be satisfied for the experience to be veridical. But can we retain this system of ideas once we move over to the perspective of the learned? To retain the existing distinction of experiences into the veridical and the nonveridical, we must revise the conditions to be satisfied, if an experience is to gain membership in the better class. The revised condition for a veridical visual experience is that the colours experienced are produced by objects with the power to produce such experiences in normal circumstances. This is fair enough. It is the next move that is, to say the least, far-fetched. To retain the connection between conditions of satisfaction and representational content, Chalmers must introduce a revised version of the representational content. No longer is the representational content, and the condition of satisfaction, the simple greenness of the grass. For one thing, the content of a perceptual experience is no longer a simple property of the object, but a *mode of presentation* of the property. He calls this a *Fregean,* as opposed to a *Russellian,* content.[19] In the case of the grass "the mode of presentation of the property will be something like *the property that usually causes phenomenally green experiences in normal conditions*" (363).

Chalmers is aware that this claim may be thought to "overintellectualize the content of experience. When one attends to a red ball, one does not usually conceive it as the cause of one's experience or as possessing properties which normally cause that sort of experience" (368). Chalmers answers that "to have a state with these contents, a subject need not deploy a concept with those contents" (368). I agree that when one attends to a red ball, one usually gets the sort of experience normally caused by a red ball. I also agree that on a second pass one can recognize that this sort of experience is normally caused by a red ball. Chalmers is trying to insert something between the mere fact of the causal connection and the

18 For Chalmers, "A representational content of a perceptual experience is a condition of satisfaction of the experience," 382.

19 Chalmers wishes to exploit Frege's distinction between the sense of a sign and the object it denotes. The sense of the sign is the mode of presentation of the object, as when the planet Venus is denoted through the mode of presentation "the evening star."

explicit recognition of this fact that is the basis of the second pass. The mere fact of causal connection is not enough; the explicit cognition of this fact, using concepts, is too much.

When we move to the world of the second pass, the learned reduce our experiences to effects produced in us by external causes; these effects have a phenomenal character, but their representative function drops out. Experiences are no longer cognitions, and they are representations only in the sense that effects represent the causes that produce them in virtue of the information transmitted.

The learned get into deep trouble if they *deny* that experience has the cognitive function that they can *ignore* at the level of the second pass. Through this abstraction from the cognitive function of experience the supporters of the traditional theory boxed themselves into a corner, from which I had to extricate them by cracking open the concept of causality. But if we attend merely to the phenomenal character of our experience, as we must if we are to make inferences to their external causes, the experiences themselves will be neither veridical nor nonveridical. Right or wrong comes in with the inferences. At worst, experiences may be misleading, but if we are misled, this happens when we make the inference. Thus the technical apparatus that has been introduced to handle the way the vulgar think about their sense experiences (with its distinction between the veridical and the nonveridical) cannot be extended to incorporate the scientific facts that energized the traditional causal representative theory of perception. Moving to the perspective of the learned, we no longer have the idea of the veridical to permit the introduction of a second stage with a more complex form of representational content, built into the perceptual experience itself.

Chalmers adopted heroic measures, because he was in the grip of the widespread belief that we can distinguish the phenomenal and the representative content of experience only if we tie its representative content to its conditions of satisfaction. When the learned, such as Locke and his friends, appeared on the scene, this mandated a change in the conditions of satisfaction associated with the veridical ascription of secondary qualities. If representational content is tied to conditions of satisfaction, this will mandate an associated change in the representational content of the experience. Chalmers makes a valiant attempt to explain the nature of this change, but it is hard to believe that he comes even close to success. It is more plausible to believe that the representational content of experience does not change, when we initiate the second pass to infer external causes from our sensations.

The theory of perception I have developed in this book allows me to sever the tie between representational content and conditions of satisfaction, because sense experiences are understood as essentially cognitive representations constructed with the purpose of representing reality. The phenomenal character of the experiences is introduced by abstracting from the representative function of experiences in order to treat them as mere impressions, which are distinct existences causally related to their antecedents. In the conceptual scheme operated by the learned, the representative character of the sense experiences is ignored. They are reduced to sensations, which are neither veridical nor nonveridical. Normative distinctions are transferred to the judgments which assign causes to the given sensations. There is no reason to think that the representative character of the sense experiences, which is a character ignored by the learned, will be changed as a result of their activities

Although I disagree with the *way* Chalmers attempts to integrate the scientific evidence into his general theory of perception, I give him due credit for facing up to the problem, which most people push to the side. This is in itself an important contribution. The source of the difficulties Chalmers encounters is his attempt to reconcile the scientific evidence with the contemporary theory of perception that rests so heavily on the distinction between the veridical and the nonveridical. Certainly, the existence of the distinction is a solid indicator that there is more to sense experience than its phenomenal character. But the idea of the veridical is not as fundamental as the idea that the function of sense experience is to represent the environment, and guide behaviour. The idea of the veridical comes in when we recognize that our representation of reality is sometimes less than perfect. Our world is not the world of Eden in which we experience only what is really there.[20] The idea of the veridical has its bite in the conceptual scheme operated by the vulgar, but it loses its grip once the learned transcend this scheme. This is no disaster, so long as we retain the notion that the function of sense experience is to represent reality, somehow or other.

---

20 One problem with this approach, already mentioned in chapter 10, section 1, is that it uses the fall from perfection to introduce a black-and-white contrast between right and wrong. The veridical is right, the nonveridical is wrong. A more reasonable account is to distinguish representations as good or bad, or perhaps better or worse.

Bibliography

Aaron, Richard I. *John Locke.* Third edition. Oxford: Clarendon Press, 1971.

Ayer, A.J. *The Foundations of Empirical Knowledge.* London: Macmillan, 1940.

Bonner, Charles. *Essai de Psychologie.* Leyden: E. Luzac, 1754.

Bradley, F.H. *Principles of Logic.* Oxford: Clarendon Press, 1883, second edition, 1922.

– *Appearance and Reality.* Second edition, revised. Oxford: Clarendon Press, 1906.

Campbell, C.A. *Scepticism and Construction.* London: Macmillan, 1931.

– *On Selfhood and Godhood.* London: Allen and Unwin; New York: Macmillan, 1957.

– *In Defence of Free Will.* London: Allen and Unwin; New York: Humanities Press, 1967.

Chalmers, David. *The Conscious Mind.* Oxford: Clarendon Press, 1996.

– *The Character of Consciousness.* Oxford: Clarendon Press, 2010.

Chisholm, R.M. "The Theory of Appearing." In *Philosophical Analysis: A Collection of Essays,* edited by Max Black, 102–18. Ithaca: Cornell University Press, 1950.

Dainton, Barry. *Time and Space.* Montreal and Kingston: McGill-Queen's University Press, 2001.

Davidson, Donald. *Subjective, Intersubjective, Objective.* Oxford: Clarendon Press, 2001.

Dennett, Daniel. *Consciousness Explained.* Boston: Little, Brown and Company, 1991.

Descartes, Rene. *Meditations on First Philosophy.* Translated by John Cottingham, Robert Stoothoff, and Dugald Murdoch. In *The Philosophical Writings of Descartes,* volume II. Cambridge: Cambridge University Press, 1984.

Eddington, Sir Arthur. *The Nature of the Physical World.* London: Dent, 1935.

Evans, Gareth. *The Varieties of Reference.* Oxford: Clarendon Press, 1982.

Frege, Gottlob. *Translations from the Philosophical Writings of Gottlob Frege.* Peter Geach and Max Black. Oxford: Blackwell, 1952.

Garde, Maria Mozaz and Alan Cowey. "'Deaf Hearing': Unacknowledged Detection of Auditory Stimuli in a Patient with Cerebral Deafness." *Cortex* 36, no. 1 (2000): 71–9

Gibson, James J. *The Senses Considered as Perceptual Systems*. London: Allen and Unwin, 1968.

Hardin, C.L. *Color for Philosophers*. Indianapolis: Hackett Publishing Company, 1988.

Heider, Fritz. *The Life of a Psychologist: An Autobiography*. Lawrence: University Press of Kansas, 1983.

Hume, David. *A Treatise of Human Nature*. Edited by L.A. Selby-Bigge, second edition. Oxford: Clarendon Press, 1978.

Jackson, Frank. "Epiphenomenal Qualia." *Philosophical Quarterly* 32, no. 127 (April 1982): 127–36.

James, William. *An Outline of Psychology*. New York: Macmillan, 1896.

Kant, Immanuel. *Critique of Pure Reason*. Translated by Norman Kemp Smith. London: Macmillan, 1929.

Kripke, S. "A Puzzle about Belief." *Meaning and Use*. Edited by A. Margalit. Dordrecht: Reidel, 1979.

Landesman, Charles. *Color and Consciousness: An Essay in Metaphysics*. Philadelphia: Temple University Press, 1989.

– *Scepticism: The Central Issues*. Oxford: Blackwell, 2002.

Laycock, Henry. *Words without Objects*. Oxford: Clarendon Press, 2006.

– "The Matter of Objects." In *The Logica Yearbook 2011*. Edited by Michael Pellis. London: College Publications, 2012.

Locke, John. *An Essay Concerning Human Understanding*. London: Everyman edition, 1957.

Mach, Ernst. *The Analysis of Sensations*. Chicago: Open Court, 1914.

Maclachlan, D.L.C. "The Transcendental Ideality of Sets and Objects." In *Proceedings: Sixth International Kant Congress*, volume II, 1, 251–8. Edited by G. Funke and Th.M. Seebohm. University Park: Penn State University Press, 1985.

– *Philosophy of Perception*. Foundations of Philosophy Series. Englewood Cliffs: Prentice Hall, 1989.

– "Strawson and the Argument for Other Minds." *Journal of Philosophical Research* 18 (1993): 149–57.

– *Why Consciousness Is Reality*. Lewiston and Lampeter: The Edwin Mellen Press, 2010.

McDowell, John. *Mind and World*. Cambridge and London: Harvard University Press, 1994.

McEwan, Ian. *Atonement*. Toronto: Alfred A. Knopf Canada, 2001.

McGinn, Colin. *The Problem of Consciousness*. Oxford: Clarendon Press, 1991.

MIT Encyclopedia of the Cognitive Sciences. Cambridge and London: MIT Press, 1999.

Nagel, Thomas F. *The View from Nowhere.* Oxford: Clarendon Press, 1986.

O'Callaghan, Casey. "Auditory Perception." In *The Stanford Encyclopedia of Philosophy* (Summer 2009 Edition), Edward N. Zalla (ed.) http://plato.stanford.edu/archives/sum2009/entries/perception-auditory/

Owens, Joseph. *The Doctrine of Being in the Aristotelian Metaphysics.* Toronto: Pontifical Institute of Medieval Studies, 1951.

Peacocke, Christopher. *A Study of Concepts.* Cambridge: MIT Press, 1992.

Price, H.H. *Perception.* London: Methuen, 1932.

Putnam, Hilary. "The Meaning of 'Meaning.'" In *Language, Mind and Knowledge.* Edited by K. Gundersen, 131–93. Minneapolis: University of Minnesota Press, 1975.

Quine, W.V. *Word and Object.* Cambridge: MIT Press, 1960.

– *Ontological Relativity.* New York: Columbia University Press, 1969.

Rorty, Richard. *Philosophy and the Mirror of Nature.* Princeton: Princeton University Press, 1979.

Russell, Bertrand. *Problems of Philosophy.* London: Williams and Norgate, 1912.

Russell, Bertrand and Whitehead, A.N. *Principia Mathematica,* 3 volumes. Cambridge: Cambridge University Press, 1910–1913.

Russell, Joseph J. *Analysis and Dialectic: Studies in the Logic of Foundation Problems.* The Hague: Nijhoff International Philosophy Series, 1984.

Ryle, Gilbert. *The Concept of Mind.* London: Hutchinson, 1949.

Sacks, Oliver. "A Neurologist's Notebook: Stereo Sue: *The Blessings of Binocular Vision.*" *The New Yorker* (19 June 2006): 64–73.

Searle, John R. *Intentionality: An Essay in the Philosophy of Mind.* Cambridge: Cambridge University Press, 1983.

Sellars, Wilfrid A. "Empiricism and the Philosophy of Mind." In *Minnesota Studies in the Philosophy of Science,* volume 1. Edited by Herbert Feigl and Michael Scriven, 253–329. Minneapolis: University of Minnesota Press, 1956.

Shakespeare, William. *Macbeth.*

Smith, A. Mark. *Ptolemy and the Foundations of Ancient Mathematical Optics: A Source-Based Guided Study.* Philadelphia: American Philosophical Society, 1999.

Strawson, P.F. *Introduction to Logical Theory.* London: Methuen, 1952.

– *Individuals.* London: Methuen, 1959.

Stroud, Barry. *The Quest for Reality.* Oxford: Clarendon Press, 2000.

Titchener, E.B. "The Schema of Introspection." *American Journal of Psychology* 23 (1912): 486–508.

Verheggen, Claudine. "Triangulating with Davidson." *Philosophical Quarterly* 57 (2007): 96–103.

Whitehead, A.N. *Process and Reality.* Cambridge: Cambridge University Press, 1929.

Williamson, Timothy. *Knowledge and Its Limits.* Oxford: Clarendon Press, 2000.

Wittgenstein, Ludwig. *Tractatus Logico-Philosophicus.* London: Kegan Paul, 1922.

– *Philosophical Investigations.* Oxford: Blackwell, 1958.

Yolton, John W. *Perceptual Acquaintance from Descartes to Reid.* Minneapolis: University of Minnesota Press, 1984.

– *Perception and Reality.* Ithaca and London: Cornell University Press, 1996.

Index